weltweit
Neuer Verlag der Leipziger Mission

Ravinder Salooja (Hg.)

Climbing High Mountains

Colonial entanglement & postcolonial reflections

Extended Documentation of an online symposium
commemorating the 125th year of the Akeri killings
at Mount Meru October 20, 1896

weltweit
Neuer Verlag der Leipziger Mission

Bibliographische Information der Deutschen Nationalbibliothek:
Die Deutsche Nationalbibliothek verzeichnet diese Publikation in der Deutschen Nationalbibliographie; detaillierte bibliographische Daten sind im Internet über http://dnb.dnb.de abrufbar.

© 2024 by weltweit. Neuer Verlag der Leipziger Mission, Leipzig
zugleich: Luviri Press, Mzuzu, in identischer Fassung: ISBN 978-99960-80-35-7

Herstellung: BoD – Books on Demand, Norderstedt

Gestaltung: Antje Lanzendorf, Evangelisch-Lutherisches Missionswerk Leipzig e.V.
Coverbild: Historische Karte der Leipziger Missionsstationen am Kilimanjaro aus dem Jahr 1895, Historisches Bildarchiv

ISBN 978-3-949016-11-0 | E-Book ISBN 978-3-949016-12-7

www.leipziger-missionswerk.de | www.weltweit-verlag.de

Table of Contents

PREFACE

On their expedition to establish a new mission station near Mount Meru, at least five employees of the Leipzig mission died violently in Akeri on the night of October 19th to 20th, 1896, due to an attack by local people. 125 years after this momentous event in the history of the Leipzig Mission, an international online symposium took place in October 2021 as part of the annual theme 'Credible? Mission postcolonial' to take a new look at the events of that time and at the same time to make a contribution to coming to terms with the involvement of mission work with the actions of the German colonial power.

In Akeri, the graves of the two missionaries Ewald Ovir and Karl Segebrock are still cared for today by the local Meru Diocese of the Evangelical Lutheran Church in Tanzania, and their memory is honored. However, nothing reminds us that non-white employees of the two missionaries, three of whom we know by name, namely Karava, Kalami and Mrio, fell victim to the night attack. Two more, whose names we don't know, were captured. There is also no memorial for the more than 600 people who fell victim to the subsequent 'punitive expedition' of the German colonial power.

At the memorial service in Akeri Church on October 13, 2021, I was able to remember the suffering of all these victims and say a prayer for them. At the celebrations of '100 years of the Leipzig Mission on Kilimanjaro' in 1993, the then bishop of the Meru diocese, Paulo Akyoo, asked mission director Joachim Schlegel for forgiveness for the deaths of the two missionaries and presented a carved Makonde cross as a sign of reconciliation, which has been hanging in the chapel of the mission house ever since. This was an important step in the ongoing partnership between our Lutheran churches in Tanzania and Germany to assure the fundamental act of reconciliation through Jesus Christ on the cross.

During his visit to Tanzania on November 1, 2023, Federal President of Germany Frank-Walter Steinmeier said in his speech at the Maji Maji Museum in Songea: "I bow to the victims of German colonial rule. And as German Federal President, I would like to ask for forgiveness for what Germans did to their ancestors here. I ask for your forgiveness, and I would like to assure you that we Germans will work with you to find answers to the open questions that are troubling you. (...) Germany is ready to come to terms with the past together. Nobody should forget what happened back then. And my great hope is that the joint coming to terms with the past will also include young people in particular: schoolchildren, students, and scientists."

On behalf of the Leipzig Mission, I would like to thank everyone who took part in the 'Climbing High Mountains' symposium in 2021, gave lectures and then made their lectures or essays available to us for this publication! I am particularly pleased that the contributions of Prof. Dr. Joseph W. Parsalaw (Rector of Tumaini University in Makumira) and Pastor Emmanuel Majola (ELCT Meru Diocese), two explicitly Tanzanian voices, express that coming to terms with our past can only happen together.

Our former Mission Director, Ravinder Salooja, deserves great thanks for organizing the symposium and carefully editing this volume.

Daniel Keiling,
Tanzania Secretary, Leipzig Mission

INTRODUCTION

Ravinder Salooja

Symposium "Climbing High Mountains" 29./30.10.2021

Heading a historic mission organization, you tend to think — at least, I was tempted to think — that one's own history would somehow not be too bad. That there was a good intention behind the activities past and present, and that in all the possible problematic contexts, there was some good that had been done. Preparing for the 2018 Arusha World Mission conference, I dived into the history of the Leipzig Mission, because Arusha and Kilimanjaro, the sites of the 2018 conference, is where the Leipzig Mission began to work in 1893! On that way, I encountered two publications that shook my assumptions about the colonial past of Leipzig Mission: one was Joseph Parsalaw "The Founding of Arusha Town" (2000), and Jürgen Günther "*Karl v. Schwartz und die Mission der Leipziger Mission in Ostafrika*" (1992). I am thankful that both authors participated in the symposium.

The last blow to my self-assured positioning on the role of mission in colonial times was R.S. Sugirtharajah's "A Postcolonial Exploration of Collusion and Construction in Biblical Interpretation" (2003). Sugirtharajah shows that reading Mt. 28 as "The Great Commission to the Heathens" was a construction of 18th-century Baptist Missionary William Carey, i.e., a construction of a colonial reading of the Bible, which since then inspired the European mission movement.

From these three publications, I learned, that firstly, the whole Protestant Mission movement from the 19th century was closely interwoven with the colonial expansion of Europe in the 18th and 19th century onwards; secondly, the Leipzig Mission had a choice to become a colonial mission or not, even if (and that should not be forgotten) she was working within the colonial framework from the beginning; and thirdly, there is a lot to discover, if one critically examines the Leipzig Mission's history.

As a preparatory session to the symposium, Jürgen Günther in Leipzig Mission's monthly history-lab talked about the key role of Leipzig Missions Director Karl v. Schwartz in taking up the second mission field in colonial "*Deutsch-Ostafrika*". Though not part of the symposium itself, his paper is part of this documentation.

In October 2021, Leipzig Mission was to commemorate the 125th anniversary of the deaths of at least five civilians from Leipzig Mission on the slopes of Mount Meru October 20, 1896, as they are: Karava, Kalami and Mrio together with two other Chagga persons who were captured, and the two missionaries Ewald Ovir (from Estonia) and Karl Segebrock (from Latvia). Setting out within our tri-annual motto "credible? Mission postcolonial" a symposium deemed us to be the appropriate format for doing so, after having had a prayer in Akeri itself on October 13, 2021. Therefore, we set out to plan it – and we encountered a massive field of learning.

The first thing we learned was how to talk about the 1896 event. Was it a murder? A tragic death? A collateral damage, as one might term it in today's military terms? And did the event occur as part of an attack? Or was it a proper night battle, or even part of a serial of fights (Müller and Faßmann, 1897: 19) against the European invaders, starting months before and continuing at least until 1900? And how to deal with the martyr narrative that became visible in the 1936 Leipzig Mission publication *"Die Blutzeugen am Meru"* (Martyrs at Mount Meru) (Müller, 1936). Moni Parisius followed the narration in the Leipzig Mission's publication and presented his findings during the symposium.

Planning the symposium, we noticed another point to learn, which is also present in the martyr narrative mentioned: Whose names were remembered and traded, and whose names were not? Ewald Ovir and Karl Segebrock, the two missionaries, were named right from the beginning. But what about the Chagga people, who died with them? What do we know about them? Who were they? We were able to retrieve the names of Karava (Müller and Faßmann, 1897: 14; Schwartz, 1897: 96; Müller, 1936: 17/20), Kalami (Schwartz, 1897: 96), and Mrio (Müller, 1936: 20). The other two are still unnamed in our memory[1]. Is it not that if you don't remember the name, then the person himself or herself tends to more easily slip out of mind? And would that do justice to them? Additionally, there is another dimension to this: how are they remembered? As plainly five Chagga people? Or, though with a different vocation, but still like the missionaries as employees of Leipzig Mission? There is no end to the learning road!

The third aspect we learned about is the question of covering up or revealing. When we issued the call for papers 2021, we thought we were well prepared. In our first description, we wrote as follows: "On the invitation of King Matunda Leipzig Mission set out to build a mission station on the slopes of Mt. Meru." The final version of the call then came as such: "... near the mission station that King Matunda was having built ...". It was with the critical help of the missiologist Taylor Denyer that we understood even our first careful description to rather hide than reveal the agencies behind the event: yes, it was the Leipzig Mission that moved into the area, and yes, it was us that brought in resources to build the station. But it was King Matunda who allowed the station to be erected. Accordingly, only the phrase "the mission station that King Matunda was having built" pays due respect to his agency, the agency of the people under the grip of the upcoming colonial reign.

This is, of course, not just a question of hiding or revealing, but indicates that the actions of the Leipzig Mission took place in a very complex situation. Moritz Fischer, in his paper, highlighted this complexity while discussing whether missionaries were squeezed between their supposed African addressees and the German colonial military. Joseph Parsalaw's contribution concentrated on the Akeri killings of 1896 itself, a term widely used now but introduced by him (Parsalaw, 1999; cf. Parsalaw, 2000). Emmanuel Majola prepared the ground by describing several perspectives on the Leipzig Missionaries' activities around Meru land. From all these contributions, we learned how the Leipzig Mission's activities in the northern part of today's Tanzania were closely entangled with the colonial-dominated context.

---

1   Müller and Faßmann (1897: 18) recount: „*Von den Arbeitern wurden 3 ermordet, 2 gefangen fortgeführt, und 3 Arbeiter einschl. Rajabu und ein Junge aus Moschi entkamen. Noch am 28. d. Ms. langte einer, Uledi, mit 2 leichten Stichwunden und ganz entkräftet infolge der Hunger- und Wandertage durch die Steppe in Madschame an. […] Auf der Unglücksstätte grub man eilends ein Grab, legte beide Leichname zusammen hinein und betete ein Vaterunser. Zu den Häupten des Hügels wurde ein Kreuz angebracht samt einem aufgefundenen Bilde des Hauptes Christi. Karawa sollte von dem Häuptling Matunda beerdigt werden.*"

Two contributions will open this documentation: Konstantin Gerber sketches how "mission" is publicly perceived in the contemporary theological discourse in Germany, and Gladson Jathanna reflects on colonization, conversion, and co-option. His contribution as a South Asian theologian touches on an interesting dimension of the Leipzig Mission's history at Mt. Kilimanjaro and Mt. Meru: from 1893 onwards, not only five European missionaries came to Northern Tanganyika, developing the mission's enterprise. But also a group of Indian Christians from Tamil Nadu, hired by Leipzig Mission from her first mission field, worked under a four-year contract at Mt. Kilimanjaro. These Indians at Moshi mission station were witnesses to when the news of the Akeri event of October 20, 1896 reached the Leipzig Mission headquarter in Machame (Faßmann and Lány, 1897: 51).

Last but not least, there is the Baltic dimension. Kristina Ecis reflects on the rediscovery and reevaluation of mission understanding in the Courland Lutheran Consistory and missionary Karl Segebrock. Her presentation widened our horizons to a very specific dimension: of course, Latvia and Estonia are the two states where Ewald Ovir and Karl Segebrock stem from. But apart from that, there is a special colonial aspect involved. The German journalist and author Mark Terkessidis, in his book *"Wessen Erinnerung zählt?"* ("Whose memory matters?") (2019) points towards the German colonialism prior to the official German "saltwater" colonialism: from the 13th century onwards, the State of the Teutonic Order expanded up to today's Latvia and Estonia, and in the 18th century, the German state Prussia expanded towards the East with a Germanization policy. When Dresden/Leipzig Mission was founded in 1836 as the first Lutheran mission society, she immediately received support from mission circles in Lutheran church territories all over Europe: from all the German states, from Scandinavia, and last but not least from the Baltic States. Partly, this support must have come from German-descending Lutherans, i.e., German Lutherans who migrated during the colonial expansion into these countries. Kristina Ecis indicates friction between the majority of Latvian Lutherans and the minority of German Lutherans in Latvia, who nevertheless made up the majority among the Lutheran pastors in Latvia by the end of the 19th century.

We can not conclude this introduction by spreading out the colonial landscape of the Leipzig Mission, from which we want to obtain our insights into Leipzig's colonial entanglement from a postcolonial perspective, without mentioning the effects of the Akeri killings of 1896. When the Leipzig missionaries were commissioned in the Nikolaikirche Leipzig at Pentecost 1893, Karl, Karl v. Schwartz uttered the motto: "Serve the Kingdom of God, not the German Kingdom, not the German Empire!" This motto could have been understood as an attempt to differentiate between mission and colonialism and to warn the Leipzig missionaries against getting entangled in colonialism. But taking the effects of 1896 into account, one clearly understands, that such a differentiation, such a warning of do-not-get-involved, was rather a naive attempt, if not just a protective claim. As a reaction to the Akeri events, the *"Deutsche Schutztruppe"* brutally beat and knocked down the involved Wameru and Ilarusa people, killing 600 Arusha men (Handmann, 1897: 57), driving away women and children, confiscating cattle, destroying banana groves[2], and handing over the land to settlers from Southern Africa (Mesaki, 2013). Also to mention, it took until 1900 before the battles at Mt. Meru as well as in the Kilimanjaro area ended with the help of erecting a military station at Arusha (Müller, 1936: 21; Mesaki, 2013; cf. Parsalaw, 2000).

During listening, reflection and discussion, one is very deep into a session. Accordingly, it was an asset to have Karolin Wetjen performing a listener's position, and returning to us at the end her impressions. Her commentary concludes the contribution part of the symposium documentation. All participants and presenters receive our sincere thanks for attending the 125th anniversary symposium.

As one of the effects of the symposium, in a 2022 conference on colonial violence, I presented my research how the Leipzig Missionary Society justified the 1896 retaliation war of the *Deutsche Schutztruppe* in her public discourses. I am thankful to the Leipzig Mission for allowing me to include that paper in the symposium documentary.

The electronic letter the Leipzig Mission received from the Oviir family from Estonia is a sign that the past is present. The letter has been added to the Appendix of this documentary.

---

2   *„Der Krieg, der wegen der in jenem Jahr besonders heftigen kleinen Regenzeit den Namen ‚Regenkrieg' erhielt, endete mit der Niederlage der Aruscha- und Meruleute und ihrer Bestrafung durch Wegnahme von etwas 6000 Stück Rindvieh und ungezählten Ziegen und Schafen, die nun den Grundstock der neuen Viehzucht am Kilimandjaro bildeten."* (Müller, 1936: 21).

References

Faßmann, Robert and Lány, Martin von (1897) 'Nachrichten von der Station Moschi', *Evangelisch-Lutherisches Missionsblatt für die Evangelisch-Lutherische Mission zu Leipzig*, no. 3, 48-54

Günther, Jürgen (1992) Karl von Schwartz und die Mission der Leipziger Mission in Ostafrika während der deutschen Kolonialzeit: Ein Braunschweiger Beitrag zur Weltmission, Wissenschaftliche Hausarbeit zur Zweiten Theologischen Prüfung, Ev.-luth. Landeskirche in Braunschweig

Mesaki, Simeon (2013) 'Recapping the Meru Land Case, Tanzania', Global Journal of Human Social Sciences. Economics, vol. 13, no. 1, 15-23

Handmann, Richard (1897) 'Missionschronik', Evangelisch-Lutherisches Missionsblatt für die Evangelisch-Lutherische Mission zu Leipzig, 56-57

Müller, Emil (1936) Aus der Tiefe in die Höh': 20. Oktober 1896 - 1936. Segebrock und Ovir, unsere Blutzeugen am Meru, Leipzig, Verlag der Ev.-Luth. Mission

Müller, Emil and Fassmann, Robert (1897) 'Die Bluttaufe unserer Mission am Meru: Nach Briefen von Miss. Müller und Faßmann (mit Bild.)', Evangelisch-Lutherisches Missionsblatt für die Evangelisch-Lutherische Mission zu Leipzig, no. 1, 12-19

Parsalaw, Jospeh Wilson (1999 [Univ. Diss, Erlangen, Nürnberg 1997]) A history of the Lutheran church diocese in the Arusha region from 1904 to 1958, Erlangen, Verlag für Mission und Ökumene

Parsalaw, Jospeh Wilson (2000) 'The Founding of Arusha Town', in van der Heyden, U. and Stoekker, H. (eds) Mission und Gewalt: Der Umgang christlicher Missionen mit Gewalt und die Ausbreitung des Christentums in Afrika und Asien in der Zeit von 1792 bis 1918/19, Stuttgart, Steiner, 489-493

Schwartz, Karl von (1897) Karl Segebrock und Ewald Ovir: Zwei früh vollendete Missionare der Evangelisch-lutherischen Mission zu Leipzig, Leipzig, Verlag der Ev.-Luth. Mission

Sugirtharajah, R. S. (2003) 'A Postcolonial Exploration of Collusion and Construction in Biblical Interpretation', in Sugirtharajah, R. S. (ed) Postcolonial reconfigurations: An alternative way of reading the Bible and doing theology, London, SCM Press, 13-36

Terkessidis, Mark (2019) Wessen Erinnerung zählt?: Koloniale Vergangenheit und Rassismus heute. Hoffmann und Campe

CONTRIBUTIONS

Gladson Jathanna

Colonization, conversion, and co-option: Postcolonial reflections

Introduction

The discourse and practice of conversion are the central focus and feature not only of Christian mission but also of Christian mission narratives. In any postcolonial world, the context of conversion is always defined and demonstrated by the colonial experiences of the colonized subjects. Therefore, conversion of non-Western people to Christianity in a colonial context is often perceived as either a colonial conquest of the docile colonized or a Christian/Western co-option of the repelling non-West. Though such perception lies in its cautious focus on power, it remains ironically blind to the power of conversion as a site of resistance and non-conformism. Drawing on an example from a 19th-century mission narrative in India, this article argues that while conversion undeniably entails co-opting power, it also serves as a space of creative resistance by the postcolonial subjects, particularly the subalterns. Therefore, the essay compels us to perceive conversion, particularly in a postcolonial context, beyond the rhetoric of colonial conquest and Christian co-option.

A brief discussion of some of the concepts and ideas reflected in the title of the article would be useful before engaging with the aforementioned historical text.

Conversion, Colonization, and Co-option

Though this essay is a historical study, I use the contemporary and commonly circulated knowledge about colonialism and conversion as the base of my historical study. "Is Conversion a Colonization of Consciousness?" is the title of a 26-page article published in 2013 by Nathaniel Roberts, an anthropologist who works at the Max Plank Institute in Göttingen, Germany (Roberts, 2013). This study was later enlarged as a monograph with the title To Be Cared For: The Power of Conversion and Foreignness of Belonging in an Indian Slum (Roberts, 2016). This is a compelling study based on empirical research on Christian conversion in Indian slums, especially in Chennai and Mumbai. Roberts places his research in the context of growing hatred against Christians in India. The movement against Christian conversion in contemporary India uses the rhetoric of conversion as colonization of consciousness to inflict hatred against Christians. He brings in conversion stories of people living in utter poverty, yet living a 'faithful' Christian life. As the author says:

> *Most of the slum dwellers I knew lived with a persistent sense of existential uncertainty that is difficult to convey to readers who have not spent significant time among the very poor – will we have food tomorrow? will that ulcer on my child's leg heal? will municipal water tankers fail again to deliver drinking water? how will I repay this loan? why am I treated as an inferior being? Also difficult to convey is the kind of courage required of a potential convert who re-*

linquishes all the rituals, objects, and gods they have hitherto invested so much in, in order to place themselves entirely at the mercy of an unknown Savior (2013: 284).

Roberts documents the stories of dalit communities, their resistance, and the hope for liberation that they embodied in their converted Christian selves. As one of his respondents, who makes a living by selling scrap metal by the roadside, says:

You drive a motorcycle, right? Well, it's like when you're weaving through traffic, and you see a gap between two cars. Everything is happening very fast, and the gap is closing. You don't know if you can make it, but you can't just stop and think, 'will I be able to make it or not?' No! You just go straight through. If you falter, you will never make it through. That is what living with Christ is like – all the time! (2013: 282).

In contemporary India, which is ruled by a fascist government formed by extreme nationalist political parties and religious right institutions, such strong assertions of converted people are labeled colonization of consciousness, and they are blamed for being co-opted by the Christianization project of the West. Roberts shows with documentary evidence that the converts, especially in the slums of India, do not buy such labeling but rather resist it. They see conversion space as a space of redemption and resistance that they find in living with Christ every day. Such retelling and reclaiming of conversion narratives are crucial for contexts like India, where fascist forces are trying to dismantle and erase the long-celebrated diversity of the land. Therefore, I want to locate my historical study of conversion within the grave contextual inevitability of retelling and reclaiming conversion stories beyond the rhetoric of colonization and co-option.

Postcolonialism, Postcolonial Fascism or Fascist Postcolonialism

Postcolonialism as a methodological tool in studies on cultural encounters, history, literature and even theology has proven to be a powerful key in understanding the decolonized people, societies and cultures that develop a postcolonial identity that is based on cultural interactions between different identities (religious, cultural, national, and ethnic, as well as gender, caste, and class-based). However, we need to consciously and deliberately differentiate postcolonialism from its links to fascism. In the context of contemporary India, sadly, postcolonial rhetoric has become a powerful tool of the fascist forces. This has been so for at least two decades now.

In March 1998, the control of India's parliament fell for the first time into the hands of a coalition led by the Bharatiya Janata Party (BJP). The BJP is the electoral wing of some fascist organizations espousing the Hindu-majoritarian ideology known as 'Hindutva', which seeks to establish Hinduism as India's national religion and defines Islam and Christianity as intrinsically foreign (Basu et al., 1993; Hansen, 1999; Van der Veer, 1994). Prior to 1998, these organizations were best known for organizing violent attacks on Muslims and on symbols of Islam; though Christians had also been attacked, such attacks were fewer. But in the years preceding the March 1998 election, commentators began to notice a shift in the fascists' attention towards a more pronounced anti-Christian rhetoric. Some have speculated that due to the electoral necessities of parliamentary politics, in which power depended on a fragile alliance with non-Hindutva parties, anti-Muslim activities became a liability in many, if not all, parts of India, because Muslims represent a significant percentage of the voting public in key constituencies. Indian Christians, on the other hand, are so few as to be electorally insignificant (Sarkar, 1999). But whatever the reason for the anti-Christian rhetorical shift, it was accompanied by a sharp rise in attacks on Christians, including the gruesome burning alive of the Australian missionary Graham Staines and his two young sons on January 22, 1999. Since 2014, the fascist forces have taken over India under the leadership of Narendra Modi, who is often compared to Adolf Hitler by intellectuals and political thinkers in India (see, for example, Bakrabail, 2013; Similarities Between Hitler's Third Reich and Modi's India Growing Everyday: Avay Shukla, 20 July 2021).

This fascist regime believes in the postcolonial rhetoric of conversion as colonization of mind and consciousness. Through its fascist projects and propaganda such as the anti-conversion bill, the ghar-vapasi (home-return/re-conversion to Hinduism) movement, and the Citizens Amendment Act, along with uncountable and unrelenting visibly violent attacks on the minorities such as Muslims and Christians, the current government in India is claiming to 'decolonize' the consciousness of those who are converted from Hinduism to other religions. There are academicians and intellectuals who teach at the prestigious universities who not only subscribe to this myth but also inflict it on the minds of the multitude in India. This is indeed dangerous, not only for Christians and Muslims but also for the diversified future of the land. Therefore, we need to consciously differentiate between postcolonialism as an academic discourse and postcolonial fascism as a politically tooled hyper-nationalistic movement.

Contouring a Conversion Narrative

Against the backdrop of the above discussion, I would like to go back to the pages of Christian history, particularly mission narratives, to demonstrate that conversion to Christianity was not always a colonization of the mind/consciousness. I argue that while conversion undeniably entails co-opting power, it also serves as a space of creative resistance for postcolonial subjects, particularly the subalterns. Therefore, I am compelled to perceive conversion, particularly in a postcolonial context, beyond the rhetoric of colonial conquest and co-option. For my argument in this article, I take only one example, with the contention that this example can best serve as an epitome of multiple similar experiences of the subalterns in the context of various mission agencies.

My example comes from the Hermannsburg Mission, which was the area of my doctoral research. It is the narrative of a woman named Kanakamma and the historiography that is constructed around her conversion. Using the archival documents about her (there are no reports by her, unfortunately), but not limiting myself to them, I use the conversion experience of a gendered subaltern as text or a mere 'extra-archival' text for my further arguments.

In the year 1896, some six years prior to the founding of the Women's Mission wing of Hermannsburg Mission in India, the mission superintendent Johann Wörrlein reports about a young woman named Kanakamma (Wörrlein, 1896). Kanakamma encounters the mission for the first time in the mission school in Tirupati in Andhra Pradesh of South India. She was not the only girl in that school. Yet she alone finds a place in the mission documents — of course, not without any reason. Kanakamma was a 'special' pupil, as Wörrlein phrased it. What makes Kanakamma special? To a certain extent, it was her caste. She was the only Brahmin student in a group of thirteen girls at the school. The missionaries might have thought that she would be an 'agent' of the mission for the native Brahmin sisters, whereas there were already some Biblewomen at work who were Dalits, formerly called 'untouchables', and who had no access to the Brahmin household. But caste was not the only thing that made her special. It was also her mind. She was studious in her studies, often engaging in difficult questions related to faith, religion, customs and social structures. And moreover, what makes Kanakamma a subject of official documents of the mission is her attraction towards the Christian beliefs. However, the missionary was also concerned about this intelligent girl because of her "unstable emotions" (Wörrlein, 1896). He writes, "In spite of her interests in studies and in matters of faith, Kanakamma is not steady in her emotions. She is much attached to her mother and her younger brother" (Wörrlein, 1896). Johann Wörrlein writes in his report that his wife, Elisabeth Wörrlein, takes a special care of this girl, and he also adds, "we hope in faith that this poor young girl be a fruitful agent of our mission in this heathen land" (Wörrlein, 1896). Since Kanakamma was very attached to her mother and younger brother, who lived in Tirupati, the mission decided to transfer her from the mission school in Tirupati to the mission boarding school in Gudur, some hundred Kilometers away from Tirupati. Hoping that it might do well for the prospect of their daughter (though it was very uncommon at the time), the parents of Kanakamma agreed to this transfer. In the reports of the following years, Kanakamma does not find any important place except some passing references.

In the year 1903, once again we read about Kanakamma with much emphasis and prominence, this time in the reports of the Women's Mission. Now we read, surprisingly, that Kanakamma has become a Biblewoman! The report of Elisabeth Wörrlein and her husband Johann Wörrlein gives a very brief account of this 'appointment.' Surprisingly enough, there are no accounts of her conversion. They write, "as hoped in faith, Kanakamma showed all the signs of a good Christian messenger to her heathen sisters. She works now in Gudur as a Biblewoman with Rahel" (Bericht über die Hermannsburger Frauenmission in Indien (hereinafter BHFM), 1904: 6).

In the next report, Kanakamma again finds a place. She continues to be a subject of debate for the missionaries. But in this report, mainly because of her 'unstable emotions.' Both the missionary woman Elisabeth Wörrlein and the native Biblewoman Rahel were worried about Kanakamma since "though she seems to be firm in her decision towards the word of God, at times she shows that her heart was not set on divine things but on the vanities of the world" (BHFM, 1905: 8). What did they see in her "vanities of the world"? It might be her 'depressed emotions' that she had for her mother, younger brother and perhaps her entire family and village that she had to sacrifice for the sake of mission and her new faith! But the reports affirm that it was not just that that concerned the missionaries. It was also her critical repudiation of mission-mannerisms, and social structures. Kanakamma, unlike some other Biblewomen, was not always an obedient worker. She spoke out about what she found problematic within her defined roles. To give one such example, in the same report, Elisabeth Wörrlein writes that Kanakamma raises questions about the mission school system. Her reply is 'quoted' rightly or not, "children do not need to be instructed with such care and given up to such hardship, for God gives to everyone as much understanding as he requires; what then is the use of your school?"(BHFM, 1905: 8). A strong voice of resistance against the imperial education system of the Europeans could not go unheard in this narrative. We need to underline that Kanakamma was not against children getting educated, but she was against the physical and emotional hardship that was experienced by the native children in the schools of the European missionaries. Here Kanakamma resists being co-opted by the colonial education model. The Christian conversion space did not colonize the awakened consciousness of Kanakamma. However, Kanakamma was not only resisting colonial rigidity but was also equally critical of the oppressive social structures in India. That is evident, though not explicitly, in the next report.

In the next annual report for the year 1905, Kanakamma is still on stage. She is yet another theme for the missionary discourse. But here she finds a place as an anti-heroine because Kanakamma left the mission and re-joined her family! Added to this, the family of Kanakamma observed a religious ritual in Tirupati directly in front of the Mission house (BHFM, 1906: 13-14). A ceremony of ritual purification. The body of Kanakamma had to undergo a ritual purification to show, on the one hand, to the missionaries that her body was polluted because of her conversion to a foreign, meat-eating religion and because of her bodily contacts with those meat eaters and the untouchable Indians. On the other hand, this ceremony was an outright display to the natives that her body is now purified, and she is not "untouchable" anymore. In this annual report, three missionaries bemoan this particular episode. Finally, Johann Wörrlein ends the whole episode with a deep lamentation, "such is the heathen blindness and backsliding!" (BHFM, 1906: 14).

A Postcolonial Enquiry of the Conversation Narrative of a Subaltern

Having now the archival document of the Mission on the one hand and the body of a converted and re-converted Indian woman as a text on the other, we need to ask, what do such bodies, emotions and minds tell us today? What does the given bodily positioning of a converted woman within an archive mean? Do we hear the voice of the converted in this narrative?

In a way, while dealing with these questions, we need to first consider the limitations of the archival space. The archival text needs to be problematized, since it is a European narrative of its Indian Other. Apart from the missionary writings, there are no documents that talk about this particular encounter. The missionary writings had their own purposes and interests in bringing this account into the official discourse. Hence, the question of representation finds an obvious place here.

The cultural theories introduced by Michel Foucault and Edward Said might provide us possible ways for a different reading of these archival representations. Michel Foucault identified the body as central to the systems of organization and 'discipline', employed in modern societies, whereby docile and productive citizens were fashioned from otherwise impulsive and unruly individuals (Foucault, 1988: 36). As the bodies were cleaned up and prepared by the technologies of modern medicine and taught the correct way to function in schools, the bodies and minds in a conversion space were also subjected to the modern European process of cleaning the dirt, lighting the dark corners, and curing the diseases.

Edward Said's work had the representation of the body as its focus, and more specifically, the representation of the non-Western body (Said, 1978: 57-73). His argument was that the body was a central trope of colonial discourses that constructed differences between the West and the non-West (Said, 1978: 57-73). This binary was very much at work in missionary documents while using conversion spaces as a place for binaries. Missionary writings frequently echoed stereotypical Eurocentric images of conversion spaces. They represent such spaces as places of darkness, dirt and disease. The converted who live there in seclusion are the possessors of bodies that are weak, barbarous, unclean, diseased or infantile in comparison with the idealized bodies of the West, which were the opposite that is strong, ordered, hygienic, healthy and mature.

Martha Nussbaum says, "Emotions shape the landscape of our mental and social lives" (Nussbaum, 2001: 1). This argument is made as a critic to the well-celebrated Western notion that it is the mind that shapes the landscape of human lives. Nussbaum critiques this idea very systematically and strongly in her well-known work, "Upheavals of Thought: the Intelligence of Emotions." Drawing inspiration from her works, I would argue that in the text and context of Kanakamma, it is the emotions that become the heart of the discourse. Equally, it was again the emotions of this converted woman that disturbed both the missionary minds and her Indian families.

Along the same lines, I take up the basic guiding premise of my argument that the emotions of this converted woman are engendered in the missionary discourse. I argue that emotions are engendered in two senses. First, the idea that the emotions in the conversion spaces are constructed, and are subject to change. This contradicts the expectations of the European missionaries that the emotions of a converted person must be stable. The repeated naming of the emotions of Kanakamma as "unstable emotions" reinforces the essentialist and universalist worldview that the missionaries carried along. On the contrary, this unstable emotion of a native woman affirms a 'troubled' consciousness that cares for a true Christian identity and way of life. It is worth mentioning here the brilliant work of three anthropologists, Brian Parkinson, Agneta Fischer and Anthony Manstead who show in their work that outside the West, emotions have been generally regarded as an outcome of social interactions and as not clearly distinguishable from thinking (see B. Parkinson et al., 2005).

The second meaning I apply to the phrase 'engendered emotions' is to endow emotions with gender. This opinion recognizes that the idea that the emotions are culturally constructed undermines the notion that emotions are biologically based and feminine (Viswanathan, 1998: 43). Missionary documents flow with evidence of this notion. There are many accounts where missionaries represent native women as big stumbling blocks to their men getting converted to Christianity. They complain that, through their emotional demeanor, native women try to hinder the firm minds of their men towards conversion (See, for a detailed study on this, Jathanna, 2015). Thus, the mission documents construct a gendered binary between emotion and intellect. In the case of Kanakamma her emotions are engendered, giving her the attribute of being weak and unstable.

With this, we may have to revisit Kanakamma's critic of the missionary schools. Here, I would like to draw on the support of another work in the context of Hermannsburg. Lisa Curtis-Wendlandt, in her article "Corporal Punishment and Moral Reform at Hermannsburg Mission", takes up an important issue concerning the missionary school system. Taking the example of the life of Carl Strehlow, a missionary of the Hermannsburg Mission to Central Australia during 1894–1922, she brings a critical factor to light, namely, the beating practice of the missionaries. She argues, "The abundant archival records of their lives provide clear and convincing evidence that during this time, Carl Strehlow, like many of his missionary colleagues, picked up the cane and used it on the Aborigines at the mission. But this is rarely mentioned" (Curtis-Wendlandt, 2010: 1). She further complains that even the award-winning biographies of missionaries deliberately omit any reference to such practices (Curtis-Wendlandt: 2010, 1f). I argue that it cannot be denied that the native children were undergoing "hardship" of various types in the mission schools. Kanakamma's critique of the European school should be placed within such a milieu and be seen as an enactment, performance and embodiment of her emotional and bodily experiences. There she embodies a distinct emotional self that disturbs and challenges the culturally, religiously and politically other worldview. In addition, her act of going back to her family becomes the most powerful but complex performance of this embodiment.

So far, I have made a postcolonial reconstruction of the conversion narratives with a genuine interest in reclaiming the independent agency of the convert, whose consciousness was not colonized in the process of conversion, nor was she co-opted by imperial worldviews. However, I also want to make a conscious effort to revisit the story in such a way that our postcolonial criticism may not be co-opted by postcolonial fascism.

Converted Subaltern: A Threat to Postcolonial Fascism

The postcolonial fascist scholars in India that I mentioned earlier, if they happen to read the story of Kanakamma, might use it as an example for multiple manifestations of a conversion space: From Kanakamma as an example for the colonized consciousness to Kanakamma as an epitome of an Indian woman who dares to return and co-opt with her Brahmanical religion that celebrates casteism. It is here that I agree with Gayatri Spivak's claim that the "subaltern cannot speak!" (Spivak, 1988: 308). Did the act of going back, which the missionaries saw as blindness and backsliding and the Postcolonial fascists might see as a brave act of home-returning, have any other implication for this native woman? Unfortunately, there are no documents that could help us answer this question directly. All that we could make is a mere assumption based on the experiences of native women at that time. That is how we can make the subalterns heard, despite their given non-spokenness, or voicelessness. Therefore, I want to invite the readers to make such an assumption.

Let us look at the time of this conversion story: It was the early decade of the 20th century. Disgruntled movements of native women were not uncommon during the first decades of the 20th century in India. It was a time that witnessed a number of social reforms and cultural renaissances in India. In Andhra Pradesh, where this conversion event happened, the Hindu reformers like Kandukuri Viresalingam played a major role in the lives of women. A movement towards the Sarda Act, which prohibited the marriage of girls less than fourteen years of age, had already begun at the end of the 19th century itself (Leonard, 1991: 99). These movements created an awareness among the women against the purity-pollution dichotomies in their own Hindu society. Social reformers like Viresalingam encouraged women towards a new set of beliefs for their inner and public conversion. Kanakamma's conversion to a new religion and belief could also possibly be seen as an impact of such teachings, as could the teachings in a mission school. However, as a Biblewoman she was not only working with her sisters from 'lower castes', but also sharing the same space with them, eating from the same table, sleeping on the same floor, praying together, holding each other's hands. By doing so, she transcended caste barriers. Conversion was not a space of repression; rather, it was a space of redemption. Perhaps for her uppercaste parents and family, that was intolerable. Kanakamma, in this conversion narrative, stands in between, neither co-opting her family's casteist beliefs and practices nor the rigidity of the mission compound. That was the power of the conversion space! It was neither colonization nor co-option, but rather an in-between space of visionary redemptive realm. Now, undergoing a ritual purification ceremony for a woman who questioned such norms was obviously not an easy task. However, we have no clue how Kanakamma responded to this. Once again, we are left with a picture of the docile body of a native woman who stands as a mere object, letting her body undergo such purity-pollution practices, now in the name of re-conversion.

Here again, Foucault's idea of a political technology of the body might help us to problematize the body-politics within the account of Kanakamma. As Foucault argues in the chapter "The Body of the Condemned" in his work "Discipline and Punish", there is a common history of power relations and object relations in the body of the condemned. "The body is [...] directly involved in a political field; power relations have an immediate hold upon it; they invest it, mark it, train it, torture it, force it to carry out tasks, to perform ceremonies, to emit signs" (Foucault, 1977: 69). The body of a converted and re-converted woman is something that was made, trained and marked both in a mission field and in a casteist household. Missionaries invested in it and had a hold on it. Now, after her 'going back' the body of Kanakamma needed to be made again, purified, cleansed and have ceremonies performed on it. What happened in both the places (both in the mission field and in her family) was a political investment of the body. Kanakamma's father invests his power in the body of his daughter to show the missionaries that he now has the ultimate claim on her body. Such meticulous claims both by the missionaries and by a native man for the control and use of the body of the native woman bear with them a whole set of techniques, a whole corpus of methods and knowledge, descriptions and plans. In all these, the converted, and now the re-converted Kanakamma stands as an epitome of an individual as well as a community that can neither be colonized nor be co-opted.

Conclusion

To conclude, I want to go back to the context of my article: the contemporary conversion debates in India. Conversion spaces and converted bodies, minds and emotions are under constant control, surveillance and investment in India today. The Human Rights Forum, which monitors atrocities against minorities in India, has documented the violence by Hindutva groups and released a fact-finding report in September 2021 titled 'Christians under attack in India'. The report highlights that over 300 such instances have been reported from across 21 states in India in the last nine months of this year. It is the high time that we reaffirm that conversion is not necessarily a colonization of the mind/consciousness. Any conversion story, whether it is contemporary or from the missionary time, is not an easy and straight-forward story. It is a complex one because, in complexity, conversion finds its real meaning. As Kanakamma's conversion story exemplifies, in the midst of all the complexities of conversion, the converted embodies the resistant and resilient spirit of Christ without letting himself be colonized or co-opted by any forces. With that assertion, let me conclude my article by juxtaposing two historical worldviews of conversion in India to let us contemplate which one to uphold:

First, the statement by Dayananda Saraswati, whom the fascists and hyper-nationalists consider as their motivation. He said:

> *Religions that are committed by their theologies to convert ... are necessarily aggressive, since conversion implies a conscious intrusion into the religious life of a person, in fact, into the religious person. This is a very deep intrusion, as the religious person is the deepest, the most basic in any individual. When that person is disturbed, a hurt is sustained that is very deep ... Religious conversion destroys centuries-old communities and incites communal violence. Conversion is violence and it breeds violence (Saraswati, 1999: 13-14).*

Second, the proclamation of Babasaheb Bhimrao Ambedkar, the face of dalit liberation, who played a key role in drafting the Indian constitution. Unfortunately, the fascist regime of India today has posed a great threat to the constitution itself and to Ambedkar's teachings as well. Ambedkar said:

> *... religion is for man and not man for religion. For getting human treatment, convert yourselves. Convert for getting organised. Convert for becoming strong. Convert for securing equality. Convert for getting liberty"* (Ambedkar, 1936: 19).

References

Ambedkar, Babasaheb Bhimrao (2000 [1936]) The Path to Freedom (trans. Vasant Moon), New Delhi, Bluemoon Books

Bakrabail, S. B. (2013) Manku Boo(Mo)di. Hitlerna Hejje Jaadugalu (Spoof of Modi. Hitler's Footsteps), Bangalore, Karnataka Komu Sauharda Vedike

Basu, T., Datta, P., Sarkar, S., Sarkar, T. and Sen, S. (1993) Khaki Shorts, Saffron Flags: A Critique of the Hindu Right, Delhi, Orient Longman

Bericht über die Hermannsburger Frauenmission in Indien, Hermannsburg: Verlag der Missionshandlung, 1904, 1905, 1906

Curtis-Wendlandt, Lisa (2010) 'Corporal Punishment and Moral Reform at Hermannsburg Mission,' History Australia, vol. 7, no. 1, 1-17

Foucault, Michel (1991 [1977]) Discipline and Punish: The Birth of the Prison (trans. A. Sheridan), London, Penguin.

Foucault, Michel (1988) History of Sexuality, vol. 3, The Care of the Self, New York, Vintage

Hansen, Thomas Blom (1999) The Saffron Wave: Democracy and Hindu Nationalism in Modern India. Princeton, Princeton University Press

Jathanna, Gladson (2015) Mode of Mutuality in the Margins of Mission. Hermannsburg Women's Mission in India, Bangalore, Dharmaram Publications

Leonard, John Greenfield (1991) Kandukūri Vīrēśalingam, 1848-1919: A Biography of an Indian Social Reformer, Hyderabad, Telugu University

Nussbaum, Martha (2001) Upheavals of Thought. The Intelligence of Emotions, Cambridge, Cambridge University Press

Parkinson, B., Fischer, A. and Manstead, A. (2005) Emotions in Social Relations: Cultural, Group, and Interpersonal Perspectives, New York, Psychology Press

Roberts, Nathaniel (2012) 'Is Conversion a 'colonization of consciousness'?,' Anthropological Theory, vol. 12, no. 3, 271-294

Roberts, Nathaniel (2016) To Be Cared For: The Power of Conversion and Foreignness of Belonging in an Indian Slum, California, University of California Press

Said, Edward W. (1995 [1978]) Orientalism: Western Conceptions of the Orient, New Delhi, Penguin Books

Saraswati, Swami Dayananda (2009 [1999]) Conversion is Violence, Chennai, Arsha Vidya Research and Publication Trust

Sarkar, S. (1999) 'Conversions and the Sangh Parivar,' The Hindu, 9 November

Similarities Between Hitler's Third Reich and Modi's India Growing Everyday (2021) YouTube video, added by The Wire [Online]. Available at www.youtube.com/watch?v=6c3bCdWaJ0c (Accessed 3 October 2021) The Wire, 20 July 2021

Spivak, Gayatri Chakravorty (1988) 'Can the Subaltern Speak?' in Nelson, C. and Grossberg, L. (eds) Marxism and the Interpretation of Culture, London, Macmillan, 271-316

Viswanathan, Gauri (1998) Outside the Fold: Conversion, Modernity and Belief, Princeton, Princeton University Press

Van der Veer, Peter (1994) Religious Nationalism: Hindus and Muslims in India. Berkeley: University of California Press

Wörrlein, Johann: Briefe und Berichte aus den Jahren 1890-1898, ELM Archive, Folder AI., 2120

Konstantin Gerber

Mission - white, western, colonial? Mission in the contemporary theological discourse in Germany

The debate about the colonial past of the churches and the various mission societies, is more current than ever. It is part of a larger discourse that fundamentally deals with colonialism and its effects up to the present day. Postcolonial theory refers to a range of theoretical approaches and critical engagements with the very historical and contemporary power relations that have emerged in the context of European colonialism and its continuity to the present day. It has long left the academic ivory tower and takes place on many levels.

At the end of 2020, Deutschlandfunk, one of Germany's largest media companies, hosted a think tank entitled "One world 2.0 - decolonize yourselves". In this context, there were four contributions dealing with the topic of mission and decolonization. The main focus was on coming to terms with one's own history and dealing with the colonial heritage today in order to ... well, what actually? What claims, what goals are hidden behind the "decolonization" of the mission?

In his introduction to postcolonial theology, Andreas Nehrings says that the central question is, how "our talk of God, our way of thinking about church, or our conception of the last things are unconsciously corrupted by the power relations of colonialism and how these can be decolonized" (Nehring, 2018). Is the legacy of colonialism inscribed in the concept of mission, i.e., is mission no longer conceivable without its colonial past? Can there be a mission outside the colonial legacy?

The broadcasts of Deutschlandfunk also deal with these questions. Different people speak on the subject, and they take quite different approaches to dealing with it today. My question is, what approach do they take when it comes to coming to terms with their own colonial past? What does postcolonialism mean to them, and what could a "decolonized mission" look like in their opinion? What could be challenging?

I would like to address these questions in this work. But first, I would like to give a brief overview of the conceptual history of the term mission. I try to find out what significance it had for the Christian religion, especially at the time of colonialism. Then I will take a look at the broadcasts of Deutschlandfunk. I know that not all positions and perspectives on the topic are represented. They only show a small excerpt, but at the same time address a variety of aspects in the discussion.

The actual reason, I chose the broadcasts of Deutschlandfunk is, that they are publicly accessible. They can still be heard today in the media library. That is why I have selected these contributions to analyze the understanding of mission in the current postcolonial discourse in Germany. Well, not the one that takes place in the universities, but the one that is public, the one of the mission societies, the one all Christians in Germany have at least access to. Under what conditions is the debate taking place? What understanding of mission is being referred to? What demands and approaches are being presented? What are the challenges?

To answer these questions, I have put forward three theses. First, they refer to the contributions of Deutschlandfunk, but I believe that they are also valid beyond that for the whole discourse of mission and colonialism.

A comprehensive presentation of the history of Christian mission would go beyond the scope of this work. Instead, I try to trace the development of the meaning of mission for the Christian religion up to the end of World War I on the basis of the history of the term. With the end of the war, the colonial era formally ended, at least from a Eurocentric perspective.

The term mission is derived from the Latin verb *mittere* 'to send' and its verbal noun *missio* – which can be translated as mission, message, task, order. The first historical evidence of its use in a Christian expansionist context dates back to the 16th century. The Jesuits' vow of mission, the *votum de missionibus*, links the term with the task of taking the Christian message to other countries and cultures and converting non-believers or those of other faiths (Pfeiffer, 1993).

This does not mean that there were no earlier efforts to spread Christianity and gain new followers. The concept of mission in Christianity has existed since the 1st century. However, the biblical evidence shows that there is no exact equivalent for the term itself, either in Greek or in the Hebrew of the New Testament period (Luz, 2004). Nevertheless, Christian mission was and is often justified with reference to the biblical text, or missionary activities, which are already reported in the Bible.

There is no counterpart to the term *missio* in the biblical text. But two different terms are used for "sending out" in the religious sense: ἀποστέλλω (apostellō) and πέμπω (pempō). Luke seems to use the terms synonymously. In John, ἀποστέλλειν (apostellein) seems to have a different meaning as πέμπειν (pempein). Jesus is regularly presented here as "the one sent by the Father". In John, the sending, describes especially the relationship between God the Father and the Son. This relationship is also applied to the relationship between Jesus and the disciples (later, partly the apostles). "As the Father has sent me, so I send you" (John 20:21). In fact, John uses πέμπειν exclusively when referring to the sending of the Spirit of God. In the Latin Bible, both verbs are translated with *mittere* (Kittel, 1953).

This is where the understanding of *missio* in the early church links up. *Missio* was a term in Trinitarian theology. It described the sending of the Son and the Holy Spirit. Two theologians are of particular importance for this understanding: Augustine and Thomas Aquinas.

Augustine tied the economic theology of the Trinity very closely to immanent theology. The acting of God to the essence of God. Both concepts, expansion and contraction, are included in the term *missio*. The mission of Jesus Christ was understood as an expression of the trinitarian arrangement (Dorer, 2012).

In the Summa Theologica, Thomas Aquinas refers directly to Augustine when he says, the origin of mission, is the Trinitarian God, for he himself is the messenger (Stolina, 2008). The intra-Trinitarian mission is the justification for mission as God's continued action.

In the 16th century, a turn in the history of the term *missio* took place. With the beginning of the so-called modern era in the European context, the term is detached from its trinity-theological context and becomes a term for spreading the faith. Since the first century, representatives of Christianity have been sent to non-Christian places and peoples to convert them. But there is no evidence that these activities were ever associated with the term *missio*.

With the founding of the Jesuit order and their missionary vow, the term mission took on a new meaning. It was about spreading the faith among people who did not belong to the church to consolidate the power of the church.

A new semantic horizon emerges for the term *missio*. The Jesuits' mission is no longer of a purely religious nature, but becomes a means of asserting and maintaining power. The supposed goal is the spread of the Christian faith. It is no coincidence that this happens at the same time as the political and economic expansion of European nations and their power. First Portugal, later also Spain, the Netherlands, France, etc. Missionaries are sent, and missionary societies are founded, with the determined aim of establishing the Christian faith.

> *19 Go therefore and make disciples of all nations, baptizing them in the name of the Father, of the Son, and of the Holy Spirit,*
> *20 teaching them to observe all that I have commanded you. And behold, I am with you always, to the end of the age." (Matthew 28: 19-20)*

The Great Commission is regarded as the quintessence that summarizes the whole Gospel after Mt. (Frankemölle/Grünschloß, 2002). The Great Commission in 19.20a and the triadic or trinitarian formulation are particularly central here for the understanding of Christian mission (Hahn, 1999).

But neither the authors of the early church nor the first Christian missionaries of the 16th century explicitly referred to this, or any similar text, to justify their missionary activities. It was not until the 19th century that the Great Commission became the focus of the Protestant missionary movement around Wiliam Carey (Klaiber, 2018). For a time, it was even considered a key passage for mission theology, since it contained a direct command from Jesus that justified the missionary activity of the church.

The term *missio* has therefore undergone a process of change. Initially, from the 4th century to the 16th century, it was a term of Trinitarian theology. It described the nature and, above all, the action of God. And then, from the 16th century until the 20th century, it became a term describing the faith-propagating action of the church and missionary societies. The actions of churches, of Christians, of missionary societies. This understanding of mission in the sense of the expansion of faith goes hand in hand with European expansion and, finally, colonialism. It is important to reflect on this when talking about mission in the postcolonial context today.

The topic of mission and (post-)colonialism has been a much-discussed one, not only in the last 25 years, also in the church contexts of Germany. It is critical to come to terms with one's own colonial past, but also to reflect on current (missionary) activity in the light of postcolonial critique. In the context of the Deutschlandfunk Think-Tank in 2020 under the motto *"Eine Welt 2.0 — dekolonisiert euch!"* (A world 2.0 — decolonize yourselves!), there were four contributions dealing with the role of the churches in colonialism and looking at mission from a postcolonial perspective.

It is not only a matter of historical research, but also of reflecting on the consequences for our identity, our self-understanding, and what can be summarized under the heading of decolonization. (Deutschlandfunk, 2020)

This claim, the historical reframing, but also the reflection of one's own colonial continuities into today's thinking and actions, is formulated by Deutschlandfunk as a fundamental concern when it comes to decolonization. But what exactly is meant by this? And who is meant by it?

I have derived three theses from the contributions of Deutschlandfunk, which, in my opinion, are fundamental to the current discourse in Germany or rather reveal its problems.

All contributions seem to agree on one point. Mission is inseparably linked to colonialism. This statement appears everywhere. Hans-Dieter Heimendahl introduces the discussion round and his first question with the words, "that mission and colonialism have been structurally connected in the closest possible way since the beginning of European expansion" (Heimendahl, 2020). This statement is not contradicted in general.

But it is demanded that Heimendahl's statement be viewed in a differentiated way. A general equation of mission and colonialism is contradicted. In the historical analysis, ambivalence comes to light that needs to be taken into account in the examination. That's why Maisha-Maureen Auma, calls for a differentiated approach. But in the end, she agrees with the statement by Johann Hinrich Claussen: "Yes, of course, mission, and colonialism form a historical connection." (Heimendahl, 2020). Felix Belinga-Belinga also agrees with this in his interview when he says that "the history of mission in Africa is also a history of colonialism" (Ricke, 2020).

Mission, as the discussion of the history of the term has already shown, was part of the Christian religion from the 1st century onward. But it was only through the connection with European expansion, precisely at the time when the concept of mission underwent a change of meaning, that mission took on a new character.

Frantz Fanon finds very impressive words in his work "The Wretched of the Earth" (1961, Les damnés de la terre): "For centuries they have stifled almost the whole of humanity." (Fanon, 1981) Frantz Fanon criticized European humanism in particular. But his criticism can also be applied to the role of the churches and missionary societies. The question then is how deeply mission was involved in the violent effects of colonialism and what part it played in colonial ideology. Here, the key aspects of postcolonial critique are addressed. It is a "form of resistance against colonial rule and its consequences" (Gerber, 2021). Against this background, postcolonial critique addresses the structures of cultural, epistemic, and physical violence that were established by colonialism and are still effective today. It is an attempt to critically reorder European thinking, European values, and, indeed, European mission.

The fact that mission and colonialism are inseparably linked is also confirmed by the following two quotations. Most importantly, they show the effects of this connection, which Frantz Fanon pointed out.

In Kirsten Dietrich's feature, she says: "Mission runs through the entire history of the European church. But with European expansion from the 16th century onwards, this connection took on a new toxic quality" (Dietrich, 2020).

One thing can be said for sure: "This power imbalance (...), which went hand in hand with colonialism and is left over from colonialism and still shapes relations today, remains", as Rev. Felix Belinga-Belinga says (Ricke, 2020).

This thesis inevitably raises the question whether mission is still legitimate today. What does mission mean today? What does mission mean in a postcolonial sense? This is reflected in the broadcasts of the Deutschlandfunk series. Some of which find very different answers to the question of mission today, or of a postcolonial mission.

> *"Mission today is no longer about conversion first. I don't believe that mission is about promoting an expansion of Christianity." (Dietrich, 2020)*

This is how Kirsten Dietrich quotes Klaus Vellguth from the Catholic mission organisation "missio" in her feature. He turns away from the understanding of the concept of mission as it has been established in Europe since the 16th century at the latest. For him, mission no longer means converting other people to the Christian faith or contributing to the spread of the Christian message in the world. Rev. Belinga-Belinga goes in the same direction when he says:

> *"We can't start mission now. I think mission has simply gotten a very, very negative image through its history as well." (Ricke, 2020)*

For both of them, the consequence of the irreversible link between mission and colonialism is that mission is no longer practical today. But does it follow from this that there is a complete rejection of mission? That is probably not quite the case.

> *"It is not about mission today, when it means making the other person a member of my club, but about giving social expression to one's faith, if one is allowed to do so. In joyful sharing with others whose testimony of faith I also accept ", says Mr. Salooja (Heimendahl, 2020).*

But at the same time, he asks: "Are we still allowed to stand up and say I believe? How can we do that without confronting the other imperially and from above?" He hits the nail on the head of the problem. Is mission still possible from a postcolonial perspective? Is mission still permissible? How can one deal with biblical passages today, such as Mt. 28, 16-20? More concretely: How can a supposed global power structure established by colonialism be dissolved in religious conversation?

There are approaches to dealing with it and reorienting it. Bettina von Clausewitz provides an example. She reports from the United Evangelical Mission Wuppertal (UEM), which already recorded all member churches of its association in its statutes as having equal rights 25 years ago. "Only the necessary cultural change towards joint work on an equal footing has not yet been achieved" (v. Clausewitz, 2020).

Here, once again, the difficulty of the continuing effects of colonial power inequalities becomes apparent. The fairy tale of equality is likely to remain a fairy tale for the time being. Maisha-Maureen Auma describes the process of decolonization as "a painful path" (Heimendahl, 2020) because it is about "breaking down the claim to universality in order rather to promote a pluriversal world that can open up many different references to Christianity, but also to other cosmologies". In this way, she formulates one of the essential claims of postcolonial critique against the West. Breaking down the hegemonic supremacy on all levels on which colonialism has operated, and for the Christian religion to give up its claim to universality and become only an option. This is a painful path, a process that no one knows how long it will take.

So there is at least a goal for what should be at the end of the process of decolonization. The danger here is that the dichotomies of the West and the rest are perpetuated, the marginal position moves to the center but does not become part of the center.

In the feature "Christian Missionaries — Pioneers and Critics of the Colonial Powers" by Kirsten Dietrich, "a white German journalist talks to white German-speaking people about what white German missionaries once did to spread their Christian faith among non-Christian black people of color — and how to deal with it today" (Dietrich, 2020). These are the words that introduce the feature. It is about a historical look at the missionary activities of white German missionaries and how to deal with them today. Kirsten Dietrich's own positioning is obviously an important issue in this context.

In the interview with the Rev. Belinga-Belinga, he is asked at the beginning: "As a non-white, how do you view these German attempts to reappraise their own colonial and missionary history?" (Ricke, 2020) And finally, the wording of the theme of the Deutschlandfunk think tank itself brings up identity, not without reason. Identity is one of the central aspects of postcolonial theory.

Said already showed in his book "Orientalism" how a European identity is constructed through the construction of the "Other", meaning the Orient, and the demarcation that goes along with it (Said, 1978). It is significant to emphasize that the context of the debate and ultimately the development of the concept of identity are set in the Western, industrialized society of the late 19th and early 20th century. The focus is on the social and cultural relationships of a person to his or her environment, from which his or her individual identity develops. Stuart Hall, with reference to Derrida, defines identity through the diversions of difference (Supik, 2005). This means that the meaning of identity only arises from its differentiation from other identities, and therefore cannot exist on its own.

It is important that difference and identity are not seen as excluding each other, but are understood as a holistic pairing that gains meaning through its context. Depending on the point of view and context, distinctions can shift or be reconstituted. This means that for Hall, there is no such thing as a closed, unchanging identity. Only in the concrete situation of demarcation does difference emerge as a signifier and mark a separation. This means that an identity is not based on immediate facts or historical circumstances, but only emerges in the demarcation of its members from the "other".

As we can see in the broadcasts of Deutschlandfunk, in discursive practice, these demarcations can acquire very real, social power. The power that emanates from a collective identity does not exist in and of itself, but only arises in social interaction. So identity is not only the basis but also the object of power.

Homi K. Bhaba criticizes the fact that dichotomies, despite reflection on their constructiveness, are not dissolved. With his concept of cultural difference, he tries to overcome the rigid dividing lines of an essentialist understanding of culture (Göttsche, 2017). Culture, subject, identity, history, and colonial power only emerge in the confrontation that involves all actors. He describes this confrontation as a process of permanent reconstruction of ambivalent identities. He calls this hybridity.

Things get interesting in relation to identity when we look at the most comprehensive contribution in a row on the topic of mission. In the discussion moderated by Hans Dieter Heimendahl, all the participants are introduced on the basis of their professions and their professional expertise. Prof. Dr. Johann Hinrich Claussen (Cultural Commissioner of the EKD), Prof. Dr. Maureen Maisha Auma (Magdeburg-Stendal University of Applied Sciences), Ravinder Salooja (Director Leipzig Mission) and Mark Terkessidis (book author and journalist) discuss the topic of mission and (de)colonialism.

In the course of the conversation, however, Prof. Dr. Auma is the only one in the group who goes into more detail about her biography and identity.

When she talks about a collection campaign by a Dutch school to give children in Borneo a radio, she reflects on the power relationship behind it and says: "It's an interesting and intimate connection, that's why I outed my family history a little bit" (Heimendahl, 2020). Here she talks about her own involvement in colonial structures that she experienced herself. Later, she concretises this perspective by saying: "When I look at mission today from a black perspective (...)" (Heimendahl, 2020).

This makes her the only participant in the discussion who names her identity and thus identifies herself as non-white.

What does this say about the discussion and about discourse in general? If we look at the composition of the discussion group, there are initially five people in the room who, as already mentioned, are introduced on the basis of their profession. Their professional positions and their professional expertise are thus the reason they were invited to the discussion. Their personal biographies and positioning apparently do not play a role.

With the theoretical approaches of Hall and Bhaba in mind, however, it becomes apparent that this is not equally true for all participants. Even in this round, colonial continuities continue to have an effect. Through their self-revelation of their positioning in a social system that is still marked by the power imbalance of the colonial era, their statements are given a different status, in distinction to the statements of others. Now the exciting question is whether this difference only emerged in the space of the discussion or whether it is a fundamental, essentialist difference that is therefore also decisive for the entire discourse.

The fact that their own colonial past is one of the greatest challenges that churches and mission societies have to face today when it comes to the ecumenical movement and interreligious dialogue has been pointed out. The structural connection between mission and colonialism since the 16th century is evident. The demand for decolonization now seems to be a consensus. This is shown by the contributions of Deutschlandfunk and the voices that have their say there.

But the problems and challenges have also become apparent. A permanent, inseparable link between mission and colonialism means, in essence, that colonialism is inscribed in mission.

Mission without colonialism is therefore no longer imaginable. Postcolonial theory provides the tools and the framing for a very specific perspective on history.

From the margins, it questions the center and attacks the hegemonic supremacy of Western epistemology. "Postcolonialism is thus not only the voice of the subaltern and marginalized, but also an expression of the resulting self-confidence of the non-Western world. " (Gerber, 2021) Postcolonialism thus means not only critique but also empowerment.

The history of the term mission has shown how the understanding of mission has changed. Now the understanding and approach to mission is changing again. The de-colonial process of reorientation is happening. But at the same time, its representatives are always and constantly confronted with the old, expandoric understanding of mission. There are still numerous Christian groups that are engaged in "classical" mission on a massive scale (following the understanding since the 16th century). How do we deal with such groups? What answers are there? Shouldn't mission societies and churches make more of an effort, when it comes to actively confronting colonial structures, to confront these Christian groups?

I know there are some questions left unanswered. Perhaps these are questions that can be taken into the symposium and into the discussion of the topic of mission and colonialism.

References

v. Clausewitz, Bettina: Kulturwandel in der Mission: Abschied vom kolonialen Denken „Wir hier - Ihr da" [Feature]. Deutschlandfunk. [25.11.2020]. URL https://srv.deutschlandradio.de/dlf-audiothek-audio-teilen.3265.de.html?mdm:audio_id=881667

Dietrich, Kirsten: Christliche Missionare, Wegbereiter und Kritiker der Kolonialmächte [Feature]. Deutschlandfunk. [27.09.2020]. URL https://www.deutschlandfunkkultur.de/christliche-missionare-wegbereiter-und-kritikerder.1278.de.html?dram:article_id=484716

Heimendahl, Hans-Dieter, Claussen, Johann Hinrich; Auma, Maureen Maisha; Salooja, Ravinder; Terkessidis, Mark: Kirchliche Kolonialgeschichte – von oben herab [Wortwechsel]. Deutschlandfunk. [18.12.2020]. URL https://www.deutschlandfunkkultur.de/kirchliche-kolonialgeschichte-von-obenherab.1083.de.html?dram:article_id=489592

Ricke, Christopher; Belinga-Belinga, Jean-Félix: Aufarbeitung der christlichen Mission „Es ist schwierig, sich dieser Geschichte zu stellen" [Interview]. Deutschlandfunk. [27.09.2020]. URL https://www.deutschlandfunkkultur.de/aufarbeitung-der-christlichen-mission-es-ist-schwierig-sich.1278.de.htmldram:article_id=484718

Deutschlandfunk: Eine Welt 2.0 – dekolonisiert euch. 2020, URL https://www.deutschlandradio.de/denkfabrik.3633.de.html

Secondary literature

Dorer, Doris (2012) Der Trinitätsbegriff bei Augustinus vor dem Hintergrund der Entwicklung des Trinitätsdogmas, Wien

Fanon, Frantz (1981) Die Verdammten dieser Erde, translated by Traugott König, Berlin, Suhrkamp

Frankemölle, Hubert, Grünschloß, Andreas (2002) Art. Missionsbefehl in RGG4 5, Tübingen, Mohr Siebeck

Gerber, Jan (2021) Die Untiefen des Postkolonialismus. (Hallische Jahrbücher #1), Berlin, Edition Tiamat

Göttsche, Dirk (2017) Handbuch Postkolonialismus und Literatur, o.O, Stuttgart, J.B. Metzler

Hahn, Ferdinand (1999) Mission in neutestamentlicher Sicht. Aufsätze, Vorträge und Predigten (Missionswissenschaftliche Forschungen. N. F. Bd.8), Erlangen, Verlag für Mission und Ökumene

Kittel, Gerhard (1953) Art. αποστελλω, in: ThWNT 1:A-G, Stuttgart, Kohlhammer

Klaiber, Walter (2018) The Great Commission of Matthew 28:16-20, ABQ 37/2 108-122

Luz, Ulrich (2002) Das Evangelium nach Matthäus. Mt 26-28, EKK 1/4, Zürich, Benziger

Nehring, Andreas (2018) Postkoloniale Theologien II. Perspektiven aus dem deutschsprachigen Raum, Stuttgart, Kohlhammer

Pfeifer, Wolfgang (1993) „Mission" in: Etymologisches Wörterbuch des Deutschen, digitalisierte und von Wolfgang Pfeifer überarbeitete Version im Digitalen Wörterbuch der deutschen Sprache, Available at https://www.dwds.de/wb/etymwb/Mission, [Accessed 05.05.2021]

Said, Edward W. (1978) Orientalism. New York, New York, Vintage Books

Stolina, Ralf (2008) Ökonomische und immanente Trinität? Zur Problematik einer trinitätstheologischen Denkfigur, in: ZthK 105, 170-216, Tübingen, Mohr Siebeck

Supik, Linda (2005) Dezentrierte Positionierung: Stuart Halls Konzept der Identitätspolitiken. (Kultur und soziale Praxis), Bielefeld, Transcript Verlag

Jürgen Günther

Karl von Schwartz and the beginnings of Leipzig Mission in the German colony Deutsch-Ostafrika

Introduction

Undoubtedly, the German colonial era was shorter than that of most other European countries. Nevertheless, German colonialism is more than an 'episode' one should easily brush aside. As Federal President Steinmeier mentioned in his opening address at the Humboldt Forum in Berlin in September 2021, we have to "seriously face our colonial history and shed light on the blind spots". This is also true for mission societies.

More than 85 percent of the globe has a colonial past. There are persisting wounds from these periods that are constantly kept bleeding by aggressive neo-colonialism. The former globalization of European hunger for power, which in parts had been motivated by racist ideologies, still has a tremendous effect on our present time.

What we call 'Western modernism' today, has its roots in the reality and structures of colonialism and is deeply influenced by it (Pittle, 2018). 'Colonialism' was systematic injustice, based on violence, disfranchisement, and exploitation. It was a system of massive control and dominance.

Right from the start, Christian religion and mission were heavily linked with European colonial history. A closer look at Christian mission history clearly reveals the close interrelations between colonialism and mission, though recent studies try to show the ambivalence in the engagement of, e.g., German mission societies and their personnel in Africa. But, we are far from detecting a general disapproval of colonial ambitions by the protestant mission societies.

Usually, Africa and African countries have a rather negative image. 'Failed state' is one common keyword that describes the often weak, neglected, or collapsed governments. Such politico-economical depictions uttered from a Western perspective are quickly at hand and refer to the high level of corruption among the elites. But are we in any way better off with our 'western civilization'? Let's just think of the Panama or the Pandora Papers!

The present attitude of what I would call 'disparaging arrogance of the Western world' towards Africa has a lot in common with the attitudes during the colonial era, which were nurtured by the ideas of 18th-century enlightenment (Hegel, Kant) and saw in indigenous peoples nothing else than an instance of 'inferior otherness'. Such an attitude was (and still is) determined by bestialization, exotification and infantilization (Osterhammel, 2021). One extremely unpleasant example of disparaging commenting occurred in 2018, when former US President Donald Trump used the term 'shitholes' to refer to African countries.

The legitimization of European dominance and thus the thinking and acting of the mission personnel had as well been influenced by a religiously biased concept of ethnic hierarchy as it was defended by prominent representatives of the protestant mission movement.

In this way, Friedrich Fabri, director of the Rhenish Mission, mentioned in 1859 the deferment of peoples and nations to divine counsel because of the 'curse of Ham' (according to Genesis 9).

Carl Heinrich Christian Plath, Inspector at Gossner Mission, referring to the same passage, argued in 1867 for an order of election of the peoples: first Europe, then Asia, and last Africa (Raupp 1990).

Africa is not the continent without history that Hegel declared it to be. The African historian, Joseph Ki-Zerbo, has impressively rebutted this thesis in his Histoire de l'Afrique noire, published in 1972. Ki-Zerbo, who was born in Burkina Faso, claims that the European invasion and operation in Africa have to be understood as proprietary African history. It is more than enjoyable that this year's Nobel Prize in Literature has been granted to Tanzanian-born author Abdulrazak Gurnah.

Personal approach

My first personal encounter with and critical examination of the modern mission movement and its history took place long ago. I studied theology in the late 1970s and early 1980s in Hamburg, when the Department for Mission and Ecumenical Studies was chaired by Hans Jochen Margull and his assistant Werner Ustorf, who became the successor of Walter Hollenweger in Birmingham in 1990. In this period, many important studies about mission history and the interdependence and linkage between the German Protestant mission and the German colonies have been published (Gründer, 1982; Bade, 1982). These publications marked a paradigm shift in the German protestant mission historiography, as they widely ended the era of a 'triumphalist' or 'apologetic' mission historiography (Kamphaus/Ustorf, 1977). It was at first replaced by an utterly critical view of mission in the context of colonialism. In the former German Democratic Republic, this step had already been taken by the historian Heinrich Loth in Magdeburg (Loth, 1960, 1985).

Since then, German and German-speaking mission societies have been rather reluctant to face their own colonial past. In the mid-2010s, the Leipzig Mission started a process of critical evaluation of its own history. This process is extremely commendable and should be continued in the future. In 2021, Leipzig Mission has started a three-year program titled "*glaubwürdig? Mission postkolonial*" ('credible? Mission postcolonial').

During my theological studies, I have engaged with the history of *Norddeutsche Mission* (Bremen) and its missionary endeavors in today's Togo and with *Mission der Deutschen Baptisten* (Berlin) during the German colonial era in today's Cameroon. The latter was the topic of my master's thesis (Günther, 1985/1991).

About five years later, I started my traineeship as a vicar in Cremlingen (Evangelical Lutheran Church in Brunswick). From 1883–1891, Karl von Schwartz, who later became influential at Leipzig Mission until 1911, was the pastor of this very parish and its regional bishop. It was only natural for me to further my research about mission in colonial times, which in 1992 inspired me to write my final thesis about him and the Leipzig Mission in East Africa during the German colonial period.

The modern protestant mission movement

Until the French Revolution, protestant mission was widely nonexistent. The secularization following the Revolution urged adherents of the traditional Christian faith to deliver proof of the truth by staging missionary success in the global south.

Reports about missionary success published in missionary bulletins and numerous publications of the mission societies delivered the arguments for the 'hermeneutic guerrilla war' that was fought in Europe and pushed the traditional churches into a crisis (Ustorf, 1995).

The flourishing of traditional Christian faith in the 'heathen world' was welcomed as a healing balm for the church in the North, so deeply wounded by its crisis. The beginning of the colonial expansion through European powers in Africa triggered the modern protestant missionary movement in this part of the globe.

Colonial expansion was a prerequisite for numerous missionary activities and was interpreted as a 'clearing of the path'. Even before the start of German colonial politics, German protestant mission agencies had already been marked by a certain 'colonial mentality', e.g., by the idea of a hierarchic relationship between unequal parties. At the same time, the German Empire of the 1870s developed a strong enthusiasm for the colonial movement. One of its strongest supporters was Friedrich Fabri, who headed the Rhenish Mission until 1884. In his politico-economic pamphlet *"Bedarf Deutschland der Colonien?"* ('Does Germany need colonies?') published in 1879, he strongly promotes and claims German engagement in the colonies. From the mid-1880s on, this mentality resulted in colonial activity that included violent conquest in Africa, Asia, and Oceania and made way for a more intensive and new engagement of German-speaking missionary agencies, especially in the colonies on the African continent. The conquest and appropriation were paired with an equally 'imperialistic' mission theology and a sacralization of the historic events that came with them.

Territorial expansion was interpreted as a 'hint of God' and praised as a 'door opener', hence missionary work in German colonies was understood as a national duty one could not decline. Missionary circles were rich in voices that shared the passion of colonial enthusiasts and supported their vision of a 'national mission' (German missionaries in German territories).

All this finally impeded any fundamental protest against colonialism by the mission agencies (their stirring bodies at home as well as their mission personnel on the ground) and led to a growing entanglement of the missionaries in the exertion of power over the indigenous population. At first, however, some of the older agencies (Basler Mission, founded in 1815; North German Mission, 1836; Leipzig Mission, 1836; and others) showed some reluctance toward the colonial project. Their overseas activities had started much earlier than the official German colonial engagement. During the 'National Mission Conference' some carefully uttered protests against Friedrich Fabri and others who promoted missionary colonial enthusiasm were heard. But the early reservations against mission in 'own' colonial territory were more and more superseded by the arguments in favor of 'colonial-missionary activities' as they were promoted by those German missionary agencies founded in the mid-1880s and later.

The National Mission Conference of 1885 as turning point

Since 1866, the so-called 'Continental Mission Conference' has been held in Bremen's Villa Vietor. The conference was initiated by Franz Michael Zahn, director of the Norddeutsche Mission, and Friedrich Fabri, who directed the Rheinische Mission until 1884. In contrast to the earlier conferences, which were organized as international assemblies, the 7th conference of 1885 gathered exclusively members of the German-speaking mission societies and was, due to the new colonial situation of the German Empire, hence organized as a 'national' conference. Among the participants were Gustav Warneck, founder of the first German missiological journal, and Friedrich Fabri.

In addition, a delegate of the Foreign Office, Consul Ludwig Raschdau, participated in the conference. He strongly encouraged the mission agencies to start work in Cameroon and East Africa.

Though the request of the political authorities was at first met with some hesitation, the final resolution nevertheless stressed that the delegates of the German mission agencies welcomed the expansion of the German colonial territory. In view of the millions of heathens, new doors for the German mission had opened. The mission societies, therefore, appealed to any German Christian to gather all the necessary means to support the missionaries in their work in the German colonies (Warneck, 1885: 533).

Furthermore, a committee of the German mission agencies was created, whose founding members were Fabri, Warneck, Reichel and Zahn. The main purpose of the committee was to offer a platform to discuss common goals with the government and other colonial players (Altena, 2003).

To an increasing degree, prominent missionary bulletins promoted the idea of the 'cultivating power' of mission (Warneck, Mirbt, Merensky). In 1887, Alexander Merensky stated in his article titled "The purpose and contribution of the Christian mission on educating the primitive people for work" that education for work was an inherent goal of mission activity and was deeply anchored in Christian faith (Merensky 1887: 147ff).

Missionary zeal in East Africa

Very early, numerous mission societies started work on the territory of 'German East Africa'. In 1886, the impatient Bavarian branch of Leipzig Mission founded the "Society for Evangelical Lutheran Mission in East Africa" in Hersbruck, also called 'Ittameier Society' after its Franconian founder, Pastor Matthias Ittameier. Already in 1885, the Bavarian members of the Leipzig Mission had brought forward a motion to establish missionary work in East Africa. The board and the directorate promised further examination (by interrogating their missionaries in India) and assured them "to keep an eye on Africa and to seriously consider work there" (Karsten, 1894).

In spring 1886, the mission board received a positive response from India, which meant that the missionaries would actively support Africa should a 'clear sign from God' show the way to East Africa or any other German colony. The parallel founding of the 'Ittameier Society' put an end to the debate, and the Leipzig Mission continued to focus on its work in India. Henceforward, East Africa was only seen as an option in cases where means and capacities would allow for an engagement and if divine guidance would unmistakably demand it.

Other Protestant mission societies founded in or active in East Africa were:
- Evangelische Missionsgesellschaft für Deutsch-Ostafrika 1887, (Berlin III), later named Bethel Mission
- Berliner Missionsgesellschaft (Berlin I)
- Herrnhuter Brüdergemeine in 1891 and
- Finally, the Leipzig Mission in 1893.

The resolutions in Berlin, Herrnhut and Leipzig were made after the final demarcations of the colonial territories as determined on July 1st, 1890, between the British and the German Empire.

Entry in the colony 'East Africa'

There were several reasons for the start of work in East Africa. The directing bodies at the Leipzig Mission had continuously discussed the option of working in East Africa since the National Mission Conference of 1885 in Bremen. But it was agreed that the timing was not yet ready. It was believed, that specific financial and personnel resources were meant to manifest first and be interpreted as a clear 'sign of God'. Finally, the Leipzig Mission accepted that 'the path was cleared in numerous ways and the doors were opened' when various elements came together:
- there were enough personnel and financial resources without endangering the work in India
- the widely unsuccessful Ittameier Society had been integrated
- the violent suppression of a 'revolt' in the coastal region by colonial forces
- the approval of the colonial administration granted to the Roman Catholic mission to start work, which was feared to create competition in the mission field
- the result of the Heligoland-Zanzibar Treaty from 1890, which granted much-wanted territories at the Kilimanjaro to the German Empire and which prompted the Anglican Mission CMS to vacate Moshi.

Karl von Schwartz, who became director of the Leipzig Mission in 1891, recapitulated: Now, we were ready to carry out what had been planned for a long time because we were convinced that now "capacities, resources, and divine signs" had manifested (von Schwartz, 1893a: 4ff). In short, now the "time was right" for mission in East Africa, as meanwhile tremendous changes had happened: Formerly "closed" territories were now open, "defiant negro chiefs" had been humiliated, and the "superiority of the white man had been demonstrated to the primitives" (von Schwartz, 1893b: 101 ff).

Several publications were prepared and accompanied the resolution of the General Assembly. One of them was written by the young colonial enthusiast Carl Paul, who since 1887 was pastor at Lorenzkirchen and followed von Schwartz as director of the Leipzig Mission in 1911. In his paper "The Gospel in German-East Africa", published in 1892, he stated:

> *"Whether mission work in East Africa is easy or difficult, it must be done. May God bless his men and women [and] may much precious fruit grow under their hands [to allow that] the truth of the gospel may flow in torrents on the thirsty land".*

This very land "God has thrown in the path of the protestant Germany, and hence in our very own path as well" (Paul, 1892: 43).

20 years under the leadership of Karl von Schwartz in Leipzig

Karl von Schwartz, who was raised in the duchy of Brunswick, headed the Leipzig Mission for a period of 20 years between 1891 and 1911. In retrospect, his gifts as an organizer and leader were well emphasized. In a mission bulletin of 1911, he was praised as one "who luckily guided the little mission ship through a myriad of cliffs of serious battles and crises" (Missionsblatt, 1911: 265).

The new era that started with the work of von Schwartz brought serious change into the history of the Leipzig Mission, as the expansion into a new field of work in the German colonies marked the beginning of another overseas mission field in addition to South India. Furthermore, this step marked the beginning of a development towards a 'colonial mission', which meant that the mission was increasingly linked with colonial power and served its interests in a more and more obvious way. The reasons for calling Karl von Schwartz into his position as head of a mission society were twofold: He had proved to be a representative of the outspoken "churchly direction" within his church and, in addition, had gained some merits in helping his church to "elevate its missionary focus" (Missionsblatt, 1891: 114).

Karl von Schwartz was born on May 18th, 1847, in Benkendorf, near Halle/Saale, where his family was involved in farming. The second part of his childhood was spent in Salder, near Salzgitter, where his father had taken over an agricultural tenancy. At first, von Schwartz was educated by a private tutor, but from 1860 on, he visited the Wolfenbüttel Lyceum, where he graduated in 1865. During these school years, Karl von Schwartz lived in the household of the local jailhouse minister Hellwig. This period in the life of young Karl was obviously influential in his decision to study theology. The first two years of his studies were spent in Erlangen, a stronghold of Lutheran theology, while Karl completed his studies in Berlin.

The Erlangen period was of great influence, as he got acquainted with the so-called *Erlanger Schule*, a reform movement focusing on the revival of Lutheranism in theology and church practice. In the second half of the 19th century, this movement gained international prestige and deeply marked the history of theology. During these years, von Schwartz met the systematic theologian Gottfried Thomasius (1842-1875) who lectured on dogmatic theology from 1842 on. Thomasius was also a supporter of missionary issues. From the 1850s to the 1870s, he served as the delegate for the associations in the Russian Baltic provinces that supported the Leipzig Mission during the General Assemblies held in Leipzig. It seems that Karl von Schwartz' distinctively Lutheran theology owes much of its profile to Thomasius.

After his theological exam in 1871, von Schwartz served as an associate pastor in Holzminden. In 1872, he married Maria Schircks, the daughter of pastor Wilhelm Schircks who was also a professor of theology lecturing in Switzerland. Until 1883, von Schwartz ministered in Erkerode on Elm, where his children Karl (1873), Clemens (1878), and Agnes (1881) were born. In autumn 1883, von Schwartz took over a position in Cremlingen near Brunswick, where he was promoted to Superintendent of the Salzdahlen diocese headquartered in Cremlingen.

At the beginning of the 1880s, von Schwartz started to appear more often in public. As such, he was involved in 'Evangelical Association for Inner Mission' and became a founding member of the conservative 'Evangelical-Lutheran Association in the Duchy of Brunswick', which, in its monthly magazine *Monatsblatt* strongly criticized the liberal theology of the church and sought the revival of church work in a specific Lutheran orientation.

Towards the end of the 1880s, von Schwartz's interest in overseas mission became more prominent. In several congregations in his diocese, he organized special services and lecturers, the so-called "mission preaching journeys", which Gustav Warneck considered as "the main instrument of awakening and furthering the missionary instinct of the present times" (Warneck, 1888: 121). In 1889, von Schwartz initiated a mission support group that supported the Leipzig Mission through its regional mission association.

Von Schwartz had unsuccessfully applied for the position of court preacher in 1886. As compensation, he was given a seat in the Assembly of the Duchy. At his farewell from his duties for the Leipzig Mission, he was decorated by the State of Saxony with a special military medal called *Ritterkreuz I. Klasse des Königlichen Sächsischen Albrechtsordens mit der Krone.*

On April 24, 1923, at the age of 75, von Schwartz passed away in Querum, near Brunswick, where he had served as parish pastor until 1921 after his Leipzig years. The funeral address was held by Gerhard Althaus, who had been a missionary at Kilimanjaro between 1893 and 1909 and who had been serving as a pastor within the Brunswick Church since 1915 (Günther, 1996).

The relationship between mission and colonialism at Leipzig Mission under Karl von Schwartz

While the mission board promised in 1892, at the start of its engagement in East Africa, to be by no means a servant of the colonial movement, the subsequent years were marked by a growing cooperation with the colonial authorities and various other players.

There was definitely no fundamental reserve against colonial interests. Therefore, it seems impossible to find proof of a critical attitude towards colonialism, as some recent authors like Joachim Schlegel, Michael Hanfstängl and Andreas Kecke have tried to establish (Schlegel, 1991; Hanfstängl, 2008; Kecke, 2020).

Occasional criticism of specific decisions of the colonial authorities or other parties involved remained "characteristically system immanent", which means that it never questioned the framework given by the colonial aspirations (Altena, 2003: 68f).

Accordingly, von Schwartz stated in the mission bulletin of 1909 in a pro-colonial manner that the higher goal of mission was the building of God's kingdom on earth. Furthermore, the heathens had to be changed into people of God. The desire to elevate the indigenous from their 'non-culture' and to build them up into useful people was part of the higher goal of mission work. These people would be the most precious goods of the colonies and could be useful for the exploitation of the land and its treasures (von Schwartz, 1908: 50f). With these words, von Schwartz declared mission work a means of commodification for the colonies.

In his writings *Mission und Kolonialisation in ihrem gegenseitigem Verhältnis* ('Mission and colonialism and its mutual relationship') of 1908 and 1912, v. Schwartz as director of the Leipzig Mission makes a clear statement: he was against forced labor, as were "some far-looking colonial politicians" since it would go against the attempt to educate Africans for work. Nevertheless, this education was without any doubt a very useful and necessary goal. Therefore, the authorities had to introduce the so-called 'hut tax' to push the Africans to work so that they were capable of paying the tax. Furthermore, he insisted that there was an undeniable racial difference, and therefore the German missionaries did not follow the "bad habit of the Englishmen" to promote the idea of equality before God. Even though von Schwartz did not agree with forced labor, as already mentioned, he still supported 'forced duties' for workers in the colonies, because otherwise "there would not be any chance for road building". However, the rhino whip should not play "an all too big role" and "an adequate wage" was to be paid.

To sum up, there was not too much questioning of colonialism and colonial aspirations in von Schwartz' thinking. By contrast, the director of the *Norddeutsche Mission*, Franz Michael Zahn, criticized colonial practice at the end of the 19th century, e.g., with regard to liquor trading in West Africa.

In von Schwartz' writings, we find a rather positive attitude towards colonial expansion and exploitation. He admits, that colonial practice acts against the commandment not to envy other people's goods, but he also argues that colonial interventions had put an end to the bloody tyranny of local chiefs (e.g., in the Kilimanjaro area), who by consequence had forfeited their right to independence.

Furthermore, it was legitimate for any people to appropriate resources, living space, or trading opportunities, and it was hence in no way controversial for those peoples to take other territories into their possession. It was even a "universal divine law", since wine gardeners who do not grow any fruit forfeit their right to possess the vineyard (von Schwartz, 1912: 4f).

Even references to alleged anti-colonial remarks like "we are not to serve the kings of this world, but the kingdom of God" are just placating rhetoric. We can see that von Schwartz' reflections on mission were in unison with the reform ambitions of State Secretary Bernhard Dernburg, who was in charge at Reichskolonialamt between 1906 and 1910. In his paper *Zielpunkte des deutschen Kolonialwesens* ('Objectives of the German Colonial Program"), published in Berlin in 1907, he appeared as an effective reformer. He was called into his position when the economic situation in the colonies became unstable and when an attitude of fatigue had been tainting the public's enthusiasm for the colonial adventure. Dernburg's program was only a summary of colonial reform ideas that had been circulating for a while. Nevertheless, he was criticized for his "escapist humanitarianism". His aim was to transform Africans into "docile, healthy, and well-nourished, but obedient protégés". Dernburg, however, defended himself by arguing that his ideas were only aimed at the economic development of the colonies, which was primarily a 'tradesman's business'. The humanitarian image promoted in public was nothing more than a smokescreen to hide political and economic ambitions (Utermark, 2012).

'Entanglements' with colonial interests in East Africa

The first missionaries from Leipzig arrived at Moshi at the foot of Mt. Kilimanjaro, in September 1893. The mission board had instructed them, among others, to "meticulously follow the directives issued by the colonial authorities". In the following years, the missionaries, who principally agreed with the idea of German colonial rule, but were nevertheless ready to criticize some measures of colonial appropriation and exercise of power, occasionally came into conflict with the representatives of the colonial administration and economy (Gründer, 1982: 220f).

The missionaries' attempts to evangelize and lead new believers to baptism largely failed. Consequently, the mission work shifted its focus to the educational sector by creating boarding schools. Later, other school forms were added (mission station schools, girls' schools, and chiefs' schools), which were a huge success.

After ten years of work at Kilimanjaro, Karl von Schwartz arrived in October 1903 for a formal visitation and spent three months in the area. He witnessed a significant expansion of the work.

When the economic development in the Kilimanjaro area took place through the growing community of white settlers and the development of a plantation economy, the Leipzig Mission faced a serious crisis: The 'hut tax' (introduced in 1897) and later the 'head tax' (1905), forced the indigenous population to take paid work, which led to a growing level of child labor and a rapid deterioration of the population's health (Eggert, 1970; Tetzlaff, 1970).

The fact that predominantly children were working as cheap labor on the plantation had tremendous effects on the school program of the Leipzig Mission. Especially in 1906/1907 the number of pupils declined significantly. As a consequence, the missionaries entered into a longstanding debate with the plantation owners. The main issue in this debate was the fact that children between six and ten were employed. The missionaries had, however, no remorse for accepting the tax regulations that forced the population to work. The missionaries rather welcomed the tax laws. A statement von Schwartz made during the Second Colonial Congress in Berlin in 1905 comments the surplus of workforce on the mission stations:

> *"We utterly owe this to the colonial authorities and their salutary legislation of introducing the hut tax. The necessity to pay taxes pushes people to work, and this is much welcomed by our missionaries. We very much appreciate [...] such indirect coercion" (Kolonialkongreß, 1906).*

On July 9, 1909, missionary Althaus, the director of the Chagga Mission, made an attempt to reconcile the interests of both the missionaries and the plantation owners. In his petition, Althaus suggested three options to solve the problem: 1) Only children over 12 years of age should be hired as a work force. 2) The children should work on the plantations for three days a week and go to school for three days a week. 3) The work should be limited to the periods of the year when the additional work force is absolutely necessary (Althaus, 1909).

The controversy ended in 1911, when the missionaries finally accepted most of the postulations of the farmers and planters. Missionary Emil Müller, who was particularly involved in the struggle, finally conceded "a total prohibition of child labor" would put an end to the farming of some goods, e.g., cotton and coffee.

The mission board had already instructed its employees to stay compliant and to avoid any public criticism in order not to jeopardize the good cooperation between missionaries and colonial players (Gründer, 1982: 241f). Furthermore, school enrollment had just started to grow again. While there were 5,800 pupils in 1909, there were 6.150 in 1910 and 8,100 in 1911 (Eggert, 1970: 192; Wetjen, 2021: 163-168). The missionaries henceforth criticized the colonial authorities only in matters that directly concerned their interests.

Missionary work in the context of indigenous resistance to colonial violence

On October 20, 1896, two young missionaries from the Baltic region (Ewald Ovir and Karl Segebrock) were killed at Akeri at Mt. Meru. With them were three indigenous guides, whose names are not fully documented. Even the correct number of local victims is recorded differently in various sources (between 1897–1903 three, between 1912–2020 four, and in 2021 five local victims). Furthermore, two local companions were captured, and four more could escape the attack. The deaths of the two European missionaries have triggered a personality cult similar to the veneration of martyrs. Even today, the 'ministers' calendar' issued by the Association of Evangelical Pastors in Germany mentions them on October 20th as 'missionaries and martyrs in East Africa'.

Karl von Schwartz initiated this 'cult' in 1897 through his booklet "Karl Segebrock und Ewald Ovir: two early completed missionaries of the Evangelical Lutheran Mission Leipzig". The cult was furthered, as it was feared that the financial support for the mission work in East Africa might be affected by the deadly events. The mission board reacted by treating the two missionaries like martyrs in order to build a stronger bond with its supporters (Altena, 2003: 282f). The advertising for von Schwartz' book, printed in the mission bulletin, however, affirms that Ovir and Segebrock should not be celebrated "as martyrs in the very sense of the word", but that the publication solely aims to set a memorial for their memory "and a serious call to discipleship in the joyful work of mission" (Missionsblatt, 1897: 120).

Similar tones were heard already in the letters that missionaries Faßmann and Müller wrote about the events: "We have acquired a possession at Mt. Meru, legally purchased by contract and sealed by the blood of our brothers!" (Missionsblatt, 1897: 19). In the following years, this narrative was continually transmitted:

- Heinrich Adolphi: *Am Fuße der Bergriesen Ostafrikas. Geschichte der Leipziger evangelisch-lutherischen Mission in Deutsch-Ostafrika* ('At the foot of the giants of East Africa: the story of Evangelical Lutheran Mission Leipzig in German East Africa'), Leipzig 1902 (reedited in 1912 by Johannes Schanz)

- Richard Handmann (Mission elder): "At Mt Meru the word of the blood seed starts to vindicate: the first fruit is already baptized" (Handmann, 1912: 54).

- Martin Weishaupt: *Ostafrikanische Wandertage. Durch das Gebiet der Leipziger Mission in Deutsch Ostafrika* ('Journey through East Africa: in the area of Leipzig Mission in German East Africa'), Leipzig 1913

- Leonhardt Blumer: *An unsrem Märtyrergrab in Akeri,* ('At our martyr's grave in Akeri') published in the mission bulletin of 1924, 51f: "We have a holy and lasting entitlement to work at Mount Meru' ... The martyrs grave may contribute to 're-ignite the fire of mission and faith" (Blumer, 1924: 51, 55).

- Emil Müller: *Aus der Tiefe in die Höh',* 20. Oktober 1896 – 1936: Segebrock und Ovir, unsere Blutzeugen am Meru ('From depth to height, October 20th 1896 to 1936: Segebrock and Ovir, our martyrs at Mt. Meru'), Leipzig 1936

- Gerhard Althaus: *Märtyrer am Meru,* (Martyrs at Mt Meru'), Mamba, 1993, 101f

The event at Mount Meru was not the first local or regional fight between colonial authorities and the indigenous population in German East Africa. There was the Abushiri rebellion, the Hehe war, the Nyamwezi revolt, the Chagga revolt, the Swahili revolt, and the submission of the Goyo, Yao and Haya, which all had dreadful consequences. The German protective forces carried out 'punishment expeditions' in autumn 1895 at Mt. Meru where destruction and annihilation were the devastating 'trademarks' of the German colonial war strategy.

The 'Crown Land Directive' issued in 1895 furthermore granted the settlers and farmers the right to confiscate any promising patches of ley or farmland, even when they were already in use by the local population. These measures were undoubtedly the cause of the hostility against the Europeans. When the Arusha and Meru warriors built an alliance, their target was primarily the colonial authorities and not the missionaries themselves.

As Ovir and Segebrock were carrying weapons (3 riffles and 300 pieces of ammunition), they were mistaken for units of the protective troupes that were camping nearby, or they were suspected to be spies (Reinhard, 2013: 282ff, Parsalaw, 2000: 489ff).

The missionaries were misidentified as representatives of the colonial expansion of power and therefore became the victims of the anti-colonial resistance of the indigenous population.

In a certain way, the mission board is not free of guilt over the deaths of its two missionaries. The mission board had sent a telegram that ordered their employees to operate at Mt. Meru in order to leapfrog the Catholic Mission, which was already working in that area. According to Heinrich Adolphi, Ovir and Segebrock had been "ordered to die" by their own leaders (Adolphi, 1903: 23ff).

According to my research, there were also three local guides who were killed during the attack at Mt. Meru, and who were later buried in a rather rude way. Among them were two 'boarders' or 'personal companions' of the white missionaries. Their names were Karawa and Kalami (von Schwartz, 1897); the name of the third one is unknown to me. In more recent publications, however, they are even not mentioned at all (Kecke, 2020; Parsalaw, 2021; Wetjen, 2021). The names of those who could escape were Rajaba, Samboko, Hamdallah and Uledi (Missionsblatt 1897: 18.50ff).

The events at Mt. Meru were followed by a three-week-long retaliation by the colonial authorities. Not every missionary regretted the retribution; some approved and explicitly welcomed it.

- Missionary Althaus: "How sad were we when we learned, that the death of our two messengers of peace was to be retaliated by a raid of war" (Althaus, 1993: 101f),
- Missionary Müller, by contrast, said, "Captain Johannes was already on his way to severely punish the murderers. Yes, worldly authorities have to act in that way to not jeopardize the accomplishment in the Chagga land" (Missionsblatt, 1897: 19),
- Heinrich Adolphi was convinced that the punishment missions were a well-deserved chastisement (Adolphi, 1902: 58),
- Martin Weishaupt (mission inspector) saw something positive in the execution of colonial supremacy: "The German government is to be praised for its readiness to attempt to work with the Masai and Arusha people. We owe it to them that these wild tribes, who are always prone to warfare and plunder, were finally subdued by their iron fist. The tenacity of the colonial powers was very necessary because the Masai used to be a real scourge for all the neighboring negro tribes" (Weishaupt, 1913: 115 f).
- Carl Paul, in a more general statement: "The advance of the German power is undoubtedly a hint from God for the German missionary circles [...] When we read about the life on the

East African mission stations, we can't help but be reminded of the old German knights' castles, which gave shelter against the heathens' attacks. Should we not expect similar support from the German authorities on the Dark Continent? To enter the gates that the strong German arm has opened, that is what mission can do. And the mission must do so — as fast as possible and with all strength" (Paul, 1900: 63f).

After the imperialistic era of the Christian mission, 'postcolonial' closing remarks

It seems that we can clearly refute the accusation that 'everything was wrong' in the missionary endeavors in East Africa. The fact that Tanzania continues the European mission history as an African church history in its own right clearly proves this. Nevertheless, we have to learn our 'post-colonial' lessons and apply them to our Western Christian existence today:

The motivation for inner and global mission found in the 'Great Commandment' in Matthew 28 is only a phenomenon of modern times. A Christian mission that takes its inspiration from this passage automatically develops an aggressive and autocratic tone. By contrast, contemporary mission must be guided by a more dialogical approach

1. Long ago, the Christian Church shifted its geographical focus to the Global South. In the words of Hans-Joachim Margull, the Church is now 'tertia-terranean'. We live in a very pluralistic phase in the history of the Christian Church. The era of mission was marked by a large variety of initiatives. As a result, there are now many Christian traditions that differ significantly from ours.

2. Our theology and church structures have lost their claim to universal recognition. They cannot be considered normative for other forms of Christian spirituality. Any form — even our very own — of living our faith is just the result of an ongoing contextualized 'negotiation process'.

3. The sacralization of history is always arbitrary and biased by individual interests. The 'acting of God' in history is not objectifiable.

4. The commemoration of the dead missionaries in the sense of a 'martyr cult' needs correction. A new narrative is needed that also includes the names of the indigenous victims, who had not been mentioned in the past.

To conclude, I would like to cite the following from the Final Declaration of the Ecumenical Association of Third World Theologians (EATWOT) written at its founding meeting in Dar-es-salaam, Tanzania, in 1976:

> *"Missionaries who left their countries to propagate the faith in the continents of Asia, Africa, and Latin America ... were persons generally dedicated to the spiritual welfare of humanity ... All the same the missionaries could not avoid the historical ambiguities of their situation. Oftentimes and in most countries they went hand in hand with the colonizers .... Thus they collaborated in the colonial enterprise, even when their Christian consciences sometimes felt revolted by the atrocities of the brutal colonizing process. Hence it is necessary to distinguish their good will and the substance of the Christian gospel from the actual impact of the Christian missions in these countries." (EATWOT, 1976: 39).*

References

Adolphi, Heinrich (1902) Am Fuße der Bergriesen Ostafrikas. Geschichte der Leipziger evangelisch-lutherischen Mission in Deutsch-Ostafrika, Leipzig, Verlag der Ev.-Luth. Mission

Adolphi, Heinrich (1903) Jahresbericht über die Mission unter den Heiden für die evangelisch-lutherischen Gemeinden in Liv- und Estland im Jahre 1902, Riga

Altena, Thorsten (2003) „Ein Häuflein Christen mitten in der Heidenwelt des dunklen Erdteils". Zum Selbst- und Fremdverständnis protestantischer Missionare im kolonialen Afrika 1884-1918, Münster u. a., Waxmann Verlag

Althaus, Gerhard (1909) Briefe des Seniors oder seiner Vertreter in Missionsangelegenheiten, Archiv der Evangelisch-Lutherischen Mission zu Leipzig/Halle

Althaus, Gerhard (1993) Mamba – Anfang in Afrika, bearbeitet und herausgegeben von Hans-Ludwig Althaus, Erlangen, Verlag der Ev.-Luth. Mission Erlangen

Bade, Klaus J. (Hg.) (1982) Imperialismus und Kolonialmission. Kaiserliches Deutschland und koloniales Imperium, Wiesbaden, Franz Steiner Verlag

Blumer, Leonard (1924) An unserem Märtyrergrab in Akeri, in: Evangelisch-Lutherisches Missionsblatt, Leipzig, Verlag der Ev.-Luth. Mission, 51ff

EATWOT (1976) Herausgefordert durch die Armen. Dokumente der Ökumenischen Vereinigung von Dritte-Welt-Theologen 1976-1983, herausgegeben vom missionswissenschaftlichen Institut Missio, Freiburg

Eggert, Johanna (1970) Missionsschule und sozialer Wandel in Ostafrika. Der Beitrag der deutschen evangelischen Missionsgesellschaften zur Entwicklung des Schulwesens in Tanganyika 1891-1939, Bielefeld, Bertelsmann-Universitätsverlag

Gründer, Horst (1982) Christliche Mission und deutscher Imperialismus 1884-1914. Eine politische Geschichte ihrer Beziehungen während der deutschen Kolonialzeit (1884-1914) unter besonderer Berücksichtigung Afrikas und Chinas, Paderborn, Verlag Ferdinand Schöningh

Günther, Jürgen (1985, 1991) Mission im kolonialen Kontext Beiträge zur Geschichte der Mission der deutschen Baptisten in Kamerun 1891 – 1914, Hamburg (Magisterschrift Universität Hamburg / MS), veröffentlicht als Band 2 bei edition initiative schalom, Burgdorf

Günther, Jürgen (1996) Schwartz, Karl (Carl) von, Dr. in: H.-R. Jarck/G. Scheel, Braunschweigisches Biographisches Lexikon. 19. und 20. Jahrhundert, Hannover, Verlag der Hahnschen Buchhandlung

Handmann, Richard (1912) Das 75jährige Jubiläum der evangelisch-lutherischen Mission zu Leipzig, in: Allgemeine Missions-Zeitschrift, Bertelsmann Verlag Gütersloh, 3ff

Hanfstängl, Michael (2008) „Niemand kann zwei Herren dienen", Mission und Kolonialismus sind nicht zwei Seiten einer Medaille, in: Jahresbericht 2007/2008 des Leipziger Missionswerkes, Leipzig

Kamphausen, Erhard; Ustorf, Werner (1977) Deutsche Missionsgeschichtsschreibung. Anamnese einer Fehlentwicklung in: Verkündigung und Forschung 2/1977, Gütersloher Verlagshaus, 2ff

Karsten, Hermann (1894) Die Geschichte der evangelisch-lutherischen Mission zu Leipzig von ihrer Entstehung bis auf die Gegenwart dargestellt, 2. Teil, Güstrow, Opitz

Kecke, Andreas (2020) Die aufgegangene Saat. Die Anfänge der Leipziger Mission am Kilimanjaro, Leipzig, weltweit – Neuer Verlag der Leipziger Mission

Kolonialkongress (1906) Verhandlungen des Deutschen Kolonialkongresses 1905 zu Berlin am 6., 7. und 8. Oktober 1905, Berlin, Verlag Dietrich Reimer

Loth, Heinrich (1960) Kolonialismus unter der Kutte, Berlin, Dietz Verlag

Loth, Heinrich (1985) Zwischen Gott und Kattun. Die Berliner Konferenz 1884/85 zur Aufteilung Afrikas und die Kolonialismuskritik christlicher Missionen, Berlin, Union Verlag

Merensky, Alexander (1887) Welches Interesse und welchen Anteil hat die Mission an der Erziehung der Naturvölker zur Arbeit, in: Allgemeine Missions-Zeitschrift 1887, Bertelsmann Verlag Gütersloh, 147ff

Missionsblatt (1891/1897/1911) Evangelisch-Lutherisches Missionsblatt, Leipzig, Verlag der Ev.-Luth. Mission

Müller, Emil (1936) „Aus der Tiefe in die Höh". 20. Oktober 1896-1963. Segebrock und Ovir, unsere Blutzeugen am Meru, Leipzig, Verlag der Ev.-Luth. Mission

Osterhammel, Jürgen; Jansen, Jan.C. (2012) Kolonialismus. Geschichte, Formen, Folgen, München, Verlag C.H. Beck

Parsalaw, Joseph W. (2000) The Founding of Arusha Town, in: van der Heyden, U. / Becher, J. (Hg.), Mission und Gewalt. Der Umgang christlicher Mission mit Gewalt und die Ausbreitung des Christentums in Afrika und Asien in der Zeit von 1792 bis 1918/19, Stuttgart, Franz Steiner Verlag, 489ff

Parsalaw, Joseph W. (2021) Als Spione der Kolonialmacht verdächtigt. Hintergründe zum tödlichen Überfall am Mount Meru vor 125 Jahren, in: Kirche weltweit 3/2021

Paul, Carl (1892) Das Evangelium in Deutsch-Ostafrika: eine zeitgeschichtliche Studie, Leipzig, Wallmann

Paul, Carl (1900) Die Mission in unseren Kolonien (2. Band: Deutsch-Ostafrika 1), Leipzig, Verlag Fr. Richter

Pittl, Sebastian (2018) Für eine „Globalisierung der Hoffnung". Zur Relevanz postkolonialen Denkens für Theologie und Missionswissenschaft, in: Pittl, S. (Hg.), Theologie und Postkolonisation: Ansätze – Herausforderungen – Perspektiven, Regensburg, Verlag Friedrich Pustet, 9ff

Raupp, Werner (Hg.) (1990) Mission in Quellentexten, Erlangen, Verlag der Evangelisch-Lutherischen Mission / Bad Liebenzell, Verlag der Liebenzeller Mission, 348ff

Reinhard, Wolfgang (2013) Der Missionar, in: Zimmerer, Jürgen (Hg.), Kein Platz an der Sonne: Erinnerungsorte der deutschen Kolonialgeschichte, Frankfurt/M, Campus Verlag, 282ff

Schlegel, Joachim (1991) Mission – Gerechtigkeit – Partnerschaft, in: Ahrens, Theodor (Hg.), Vom Gehorsam des Glaubens, Ammersbek, Verlag an der Lottbek Peter Jensen, 161ff von Schwartz, Karl (1893a) Ein neues Feld unserer Missionsarbeit, in: Evangelisch-Lutherisches Missionsblatt, Leipzig, Verlag der Ev.-Luth. Mission, 4ff

von Schwartz, Karl (1893b) Evangelische Missionstätigkeit in Ostafrika, in: Evangelisch-Lutherisches Missionsblatt, Leipzig, Verlag der Ev.-Luth. Mission, 101ff

von Schwartz, Karl (1897) Karl Segebrock und Ewald Ovir: zwei früh vollendete Missionare der Evangelisch-lutherischen Mission zu Leipzig, Leipzig, Verlag der Ev.-Luth. Mission

von Schwartz, Karl (1908) Stand, Aufgaben und Aussichten der Mission in Deutsch-Ostafrika, in: Evangelisch-Lutherisches Missionsblatt, Leipzig, Verlag der Ev.-Luth. Mission, 49ff

von Schwartz, Karl (1912) Mission und Kolonisation in ihrem gegenseitigen Verhältnis. Missionsstudie (2. Auflage), Leipzig, Verlag der Ev.-Luth. Mission

Tetzlaff, Rainer (1970) Koloniale Entwicklung und Ausbeutung. Wirtschafts- und Sozialgeschichte Deutsch-Ostafrikas 1885-1914, Berlin, Duncker & Humblot

Ustorf, Werner (1995) Die Diskussion der Missionsgeschichte im Protestantismus seit dem 16. Jahrhundert, in: Müller, K. / Ustorf, W., Einleitung in die Missionsgeschichte. Tradition, Situation und Dynamik des Christentums, Stuttgart, Berlin, Köln, Verlag W. Kohlhammer, 11ff

Utermark, Sören (2012) „Schwarzer Untertan versus schwarzer Bruder". Bernhard Dernburgs Reformen in den Kolonien Deutsch-Ostafrika, Deutsch-Südwestafrika, Togo und Kamerun, Kassel, Universitätsbibliothek

Warneck, Gustav (1885) Eine bedeutsame Missions-Konferenz, in: Allgemeine Missions-Zeitschrift, Bertelsmann Verlag Gütersloh, 545ff

Warneck, Gustav (1888) Kirchenmission oder Freie Mission? Eine Antwort auf die Frage: In wieweit ist die Eingliederung der Mission in den amtskirchlichen Organismus berechtigt oder ausführbar? in: Allgemeine Missions-Zeitschrift 1888, Bertelsmann Verlag Gütersloh, 121ff

Weishaupt, Martin (1913) Ostafrikanische Wandertage. Durch das Gebiet der Leipziger Mission in Deutsch-Ostafrika, Leipzig: Verlag der Ev.-Luth. Mission

Wetjen, Karolin (2021) Mission als theologisches Labor. Koloniale Aushandlungen des Religiösen in Ostafrika um 1900, Stuttgart, Franz Steiner Verlag

Moritz Fischer

Inevitably drawn into the machinery of war? An entanglement-analytical perspective on Leipzig missionaries, caught between their African addressees and the German colonial military"

With the following contribution, I would like to take on the task, outlined by the question, "What discursive entanglements can be discerned from the historiography of the supposedly tragic events on the night of October 19-20, 1896, in Akeri on the slopes of Mount Meru in East Africa (today Tanzania)?" We want to look at the different actors, factors, spaces, and networks of mission and productively include them in an analysis that goes beyond the dichotomy of foreign colonization and mission versus indigenous reaction. In doing so, it is important to follow a perspective that asks about historical interconnections and entanglements. A history of entanglements, on the one hand, emphasizes commonalities and mutual relationships so that tunnel vision is overcome in explaining the history of a nation or – in the case of the mission – of a society from within itself. On the other hand, this perspective also makes clear that interactions and interdependencies not only lead to commonalities but at the same time produce conflicts, demarcations, and ruptures when it comes to unintentional misunderstandings, obvious lies, misinterpretation of information, corruption, and strategic alliances.

To exemplify the question, I ask, how was mission history subsequently constructed in relation to the event in Akeri? What different oral, political, and institutional expressions can be observed? How can the confusion that arose between actual and alleged perpetrators be disentangled and the silent victims identified? Who were the "victims" on the slopes of Mount Meru and how are their "murders" to be understood? Before I go into detail, I would like to raise the question: "What is history"? But I will not discuss it because asking for a definition like that will lead to a never-ending debate. Instead of debating this definition, I found an inspiring quote that shall serve us as a working answer. The quote is by the US-American linguist Paul Allen Miller, "History from the perspective of the Real is not a narrative of events, but a series of symbolic systems progressively collapsing before their own ineffable but changing beyond." (Miller, 1999: 219). Let us keep this answer in mind while concentrating on the research-question: "What discursive entanglements emerge from the historiography of the supposedly so-called "tragic events" on the night of October 19-20, 1896, in Akeri?"

1. Navigation through a discursively entangled historiography

If one considers the different actors, factors, spaces, and networks of the mission and productively includes them in an analysis that – informed by postcolonial theoretical debates – goes beyond the dichotomy of foreign colonization and mission versus indigenous reaction, we will need to follow a perspective that asks about interconnections and entanglements.

1.1 What is the contribution of discourse theory to our historical understanding?

I follow herewith Philipp Sarasin, who asserts that a "discourse theory raises the question of the materiality of sources. It draws attention to the fact that the 'inherent logic' of the material handed down cannot be dealt with in a source-critical way in order to restore a transparency obscured solely by distortions and falsifications, but that this 'inherent logic' is to be investigated and becomes a constitutive part of historiography. For us, the past is neither a "reality" nor are we allowed to reconstruct its supposed "meaning" as an ideal "beyond" the sources. The description and analysis of the past can, therefore, never detach themselves from the description and analysis of the sources. It remains bound to the "symbolic systems" that we identify in written documents, oral traditions, or visualizations of the "past" in photographs and film. What comes into view is not an arbitrary, supposedly postmodern game of texts that only refer to each other without reference to reality, but concrete, socially locatable forms and relations of media and communication, of information processing and meaning production" (Sarasin, 32011: 82-83). These insights are applicable now.

1.2 "Entangled historiography" as an instrument to deconstruct the hegemonial discourse on the "Akeri killings" of 1896

An intercultural historiography of "entanglements" first emphasizes commonalities and mutual relationships. Secondly, this perspective also makes it clear that interactions and interdependencies not only led to commonalities, but at the same time produced conflicts, demarcations, and ruptures. I want to introduce, beside the notion of "entanglements" so-called "dis-entanglements" resulting in secessions, splits, migration, and various forms of resistance as creative reactions to violence, oppression, colonialization, etc.

In researching mission history, I rely on navigating through "entangled history" by examining different times in discursive spaces and between various actors. As the name entangled history (Histoire Croisée) already suggests, it deals with entanglements, intersections, and intercrossings. With this theory, Michael Werner and Bénédicte Zimmermann created a model that shows the complexity of history and historical events in a globalized and intertwined world where everything is interdependent (Werner/Zimmermann, 2006). A history of entanglements, according to Shalini Randeria and Frederick Cooper, on the one hand, emphasizes exchange relationships, but even cases of accidental misunderstandings, obvious lies, misinterpreting information, executing corruption, and forming strategic alliances (Conrad/Randeria, 22013, 40f).

With the following case study, I try to understand the conflicts that resulted in the tragic deaths of Ewald Ovir and Karl Segebrock in the morning of October 20, 1896, and to investigate the tragic consequences in the wake of those killings. We ask if it is possible even exactly 125 years after the event, by providing a specific re-reading of accessible archived documents, narratives, and related discourses from a postcolonial perspective, as per the methodology of "entangled historiography." The researcher who uses the method of "entangled history", or "Histoire croisée", must consider historical "times" and "spaces" in their specific interconnectedness as dimensions in which the "actors" act (Ratschiller/Wetjen, 2018). Therefore, to understand different actors, factors, spaces, and networks of the mission in productive analysis, informed by postcolonial theoretical debates, one must go beyond the dichotomy of foreign colonization and mission vs. indigenous reactions. Instead, it is better to follow a perspective that examines the interconnections (entanglements) in the situation.

1.3 Research-objectives, put in order according to the presentation's fourfold structure:

We will have to...
1. ... deconstruct and even re-construct the contextual situation of Segebrock and Ovir towards the various actors on the night of October 19-20, 1896.
2. ... find out the main motives of the involved political German as well as African actors in a process that resulted in the deaths of Segebrock and Ovir.
3. ... make visible the entanglements of power relationships between the Leipzig Mission and an African leadership caught between resistance to missionary work and cooperation with it.
4. ... define guidelines for a postcolonial understanding of the entangled history of mission at the interface of interrelated churches and Christians from the global "North" and "South."

1.4 The "Colonial Situation" (G. Balandier) and "The Origins of Totalitarianism" (H. Arendt)

According to Balandier, the colonial situation describes a system in which the white colonizing minority, with absolute power based on brutal force, mercilessly enforces its political and economic goals against the black minority. The world of the colonized and the colonial masters reveals antagonisms that follow the principle of mutual exclusion. The boundaries between black and white are constituted by the power of the military, the police, and the guns of the settlers. The colonial situation is almost Manichean in character; there can be no dialogue or reconciliation between masters and servants. The colonial situation is reinforced by ideological and religious patterns. The colonized are denied their humanity; they are degraded to savage and manipulable "things." Their lives are determined by the iron laws of racism. The colonial situation is the framework in which white missionaries and black Christians confront each other. In my work, I start here and attempt to give back dignity in my historical narration. It somewhat aligns with subaltern studies.

In part two of "The Origins of Totalitarianism", Hannah Arendt investigates scientific racism and its role in colonialist imperialism, itself characterized by unlimited territorial and economic expansion (Arendt, 1986). That unlimited expansion necessarily opposed itself and was hostile to the territorially delimited nation-state. Arendt traces the roots of modern imperialism to the accumulation of excess capital in European nation-states during the 19th century. This capital required overseas investments outside of Europe to be productive, and political control had to be expanded overseas to protect the investments. She then examines "continental imperialism" (pan-Germanism and pan-Slavism) and the emergence of "movements" substituting themselves for the political parties. These movements were hostile to the state and anti-parliamentary, and they gradually institutionalized anti-Semitism and other kinds of racism.

2. Factors and actors in certain times at certain places related to the "events" of October 20, 1896

The "dry facts" of the "Akeri killings" (Parsalaw, 1999: 66ff) which resulted in an influential missionary as well as colonial "narrative", are: In the dark morning hours of October 20, 1896, Ewald Ovir and Karl Segebrock, pioneer-missionaries of the Leipzig Mission, spend the first night in a provisory camp on the plot of land they had bought at Akeri on the slopes of Mt. Meru for the founding of a new mission station. They had brought with them big loads of needed equipment to establish the mission, even three rifles, given by Captain Kurt Johannes of the German protecting army ("*Schutztruppe*"). Johannes was intentionally passing by Akeri on a military exposure-tour to Mbugwe in the west, traveling together with his young wife, Amelie Johannes, and a unit of soldiers. The small colonial army stayed the same night within 800 meters of the Akeri-camp with the idea of looking after the right. What happened was a first contact with Arusha warriors who, "rattling the sabers", had surrounded the camp of the "*Schutztruppe*" who reacted by firing heavily into the night (Spear, 1997: 70-71). The warriors moved further and attacked the missionaries in their provisional camp, killing them with spears along with three Chagga assistants. They fired at least one shot. Due to the earlier raids of Captain Johannes and his troops against the Arusha in 1895, they mistakenly considered them defeated.

There are several reports, documents, official statements, and later publications on this event.[3] Each one is more or less tendentious and guided by certain interests, including false propaganda and political indoctrination. I cannot investigate all of these documents in detail, which is not my purpose here and would require a detailed discourse analysis of the publications themselves. We can identify three types of publications: mission magazines, reports by missionaries, and magazines of the late 1960s onward showing the awakening self-aware-

---

1   Comp. Müller, Faßmann, 1897. Die Bluttaufe unserer Mission am Meru. Nach Briefen von Müller und Faßmann, in: Evangelisch-Lutherisches Missionsblatt (= ELMB), 12-19; Schwartz, 1897, Karl Segebrock und Ewald Ovir. Zwei früh vollendete Missionare der Evangelisch-lutherischen Mission zu Leipzig, Leipzig; Parsalaw, 1999, A History of the Church, Diocese in the Arusha Region from 1904 to 1958, Erlangen, 66ff; Groop, 2006, With the Gospel to Maasailand. Lutheran Mission Work among the Arusha and Maasai in Northern Tanzania 1904-1973. Abo, 39-49; Parsalaw, 2000, The Founding of Arusha Town, in: Heyden (eds.). Mission und Gewalt. Der Umgang christlicher Missionen mit Gewalt und die Ausbreitung des Christentums in Afrika und Asien in der Zeit von 1792-1918/19, Stuttgart, 489-493; Altena, 2003, „Ein Häuflein Christen mitten in der Heidenwelt des dunklen Erdteils". Zum Selbst- und Fremdverständnis protestantischer Missionare im kolonialen Afrika 1884-1918. Münster, 282-284; Althaus, 1992, Mamba. Anfang in Afrika, (bearbeitet und hrsg. von Hans-Ludwig Althaus). Erlangen (Kap. 31: „Märtyrer am Meru", 101-102); Müller, 1936, Aus der Tiefe in die Höh', 20. Oktober 1896-1936. Segebrock und Ovir, unsere Blutzeugen am Meru, Leipzig; Schwartz, 1912, Mission und Kolonisation in ihrem gegenseitigen Verhältnis. Missionsstudie, Leipzig; Spear, 1997, Mountain Farmers. Moral Economies of Land & Agricultural Development in Arusha & Meru. Oxford / Dar es Salaam

ness of Tanzanian Christianity itself.[4] These are all written in Kiswahili, the African lingua franca of Tanzania.[5] Two sources are publications in two church magazines (1969 / 1971), which describe the event more generally.[6] And lastly, modern research from a postcolonial and historically critical perspective. The third of these documents is written (in Kiswahili) by typewriter, the "History of the Evangelical-Lutheran Church in Tanzania 1893-1940" by Kiesel[7] and the last one is the documentation of "oral history" by Matthayo Kaaya, born and living close to Akeri around 1880. He was interviewed by Kiesel in the late 1960s. The Meru-born Kaaya is an indirect witness to the occurrences of October 20, 1896, and reports the personal names of Chagga warriors who murdered Arusha men and women as well as captured women, which shows special knowledge. We observe and deconstruct eight historical factors being intersected or entangled with one another (there are more factors, but we must limit ourselves here).

2.1 Traditional African societies (Chagga, Meru, Arusha, Maasai) in relations

The Chagga and the Meru peoples share many similarities economically, linguistically, culturally as well as religiously. Both developed in the last 100 years before the "event", living on the rich banana grove and coffee plantation slopes of Mount Kilimanjaro (Chagga) and Mount Meru (Meru) in northern Tanzania. Meru society and economy had, at the end of the 19th century, just started to adjust to German colonial government influences. Next, the Maasai and Arusha are similar from a cultural perspective. Maasai differ in many aspects from the majority of the ethnic Bantu-groups in East-Africa. Having settled at the southern slopes of Mt. Meru, these early Arusha colonizers started farming. Protected by the neighboring Kisongo-Maasai, the Arusha Maasai-section could dwell there peacefully despite the Meru tribe already settled in the southern parts of Meru. In time, the Arusha grew in number, economic strength, and confidence. They not only challenged their Bantu neighbors, the Meru, but also their once superior Maasai patrons in the steppe.

Indigenous military context: resisting Maasai warriors, the "Ilmurran": Maasai men at a certain age are understood as "warriors." In their official function, they protect their people, their cattle, and the grazing lands they make use of. Maasai society's organization is strongly

---

2   Umoja XXI (Novemba 1969/252), "Historia Fupi Ya Dayosisi Yetu Ya Kaskazini", 3-4; Uhuru na Amani 60 (May 1971/5), "Mashahidi wa Yesu Huko Meru", 9-11 (K.P. Kiesel); Historia ya Kanisa la Kiinjili la Kilutheri Tanzania Kaskazini toka 1893-1940 (K.P. Kiesel); in the archive of ELCT-Northern Diocese in Moshi: „Kitabu cha Matthayo Kaaya" (ed. K.P. Kiesel)

5   They all go back to the authorship of the former missionary and long-term co-worker of the ELCT-Northern Diocese, Rev. Klaus-Peter Kiesel, originating from the Neuendettelsau Mission. He served in the areas of Meru and Kilimanjaro as a con-gregational pastor from end 1960s until early 2000s. Beside that he was responsible in these decades as church-historian fort the archive at the headquarter of the Northern Diocese at Moshi.

6   The oral testimony of one of the warriors with the name Paulo is written down in: Umoja XXI (Novemba 1969/252), 3

7   In the history of the Evangelical-Lutheran Church (1893-1940) K.P. Kiesel refers on page 28-33 quite elaborated on the event. He seems to relay on the Evangelisch-Lutherisches Missionsblatt (= ELMB) 1897 and on Althaus.

patriarchal, with elder men, sometimes joined by retired elders, deciding the most important matters for each Maasai group. They wear the symbolic color red to represent power. If a diviner (Maa: loibon[8], also respected as a ritual expert and as a prophet) has gained enough reputation in his society, he might be consulted by certain groups of Maasai. According to Fosbrooke, he "provides charms and establishes a ceremonial to be utilized to the advantage of the whole group" (Fosbrooke, 1948: 13-14).

These (…) "diviners are consulted to procure success in war, good rainfalls, and help against diseases. Another group consists of the chief diviners. These loibons enjoy great respect among the people they serve. They are the spiritual leaders of the tribe and the sections, and in addition to duties they have in common with the lesser diviners, they sanction war raids as well as bless and authorize ceremonies affecting the whole Maasai tribe" (Groop, 2006: 28).

2.2 Coastal colonial regime of the Sultanate of Zanzibar

The sultans of Zanzibar were the rulers of the "Sultanate of Zanzibar." The latter was instituted on October 19, 1856, after the death of Said bin Sultan, since 1804 ruler of "Oman and Zanzibar." The sultans of Zanzibar controlled the main parts of the east African coast, known as Zanj until 1886. They ruled over the trading routes extending further into the continent, passing by Mount Kilimanjaro and Mount Meru on one of their routes and as far as Kindu on the Congo River. With the signing of the Heligoland-Zanzibar Treaty in 1890, during Ali bin Said's reign, Zanzibar became officially registered as a British protectorate. It was Sayyid Hamoud bin Mohammed Al-Said (1853–1902) who ruled from August 1896 to July 1902. He was the 7th Sultan of Zanzibar, ruling at the time of the Akeri-event but not directly entangled with it. He was not controlled by the Germans but by the British. Since Omani was the Sultan of the protectorate of Zanzibar, slavery on the island was outlawed. Hamoud became Sultan with the support of the British consul, Sir Basil Cave, upon the death of Sayyid Hamad bin Thuwaini. Hamoud demanded that slavery be abolished in Zanzibar and that all the slaves be liberated.

2.3 German Imperial Protection Force ("Kaiserliche Schutztruppe")

To understand the foreign military context, we have to describe the importance of the conquering German colonial army, the "Schutztruppe". Schutztruppe was the official name for the military units in the German colonies in Africa from 1891 until their disbandment in October 1919. They were subordinate to the Reichsmarineamt until 1896, to the Colonial Department of the Foreign Office from 1896, and to the Reichskolonialamt beginning with its establishment in 1907. The term Schutztruppe goes back to the decision of the empire's chancellor Otto von Bismarck to use the term protectorate instead of colony for the acquired or conquered overseas territories, as he was concerned with protecting German trade with and

---

8   The Maa word for diviner is oloiboni, pl. iloibonok. For this paper I make use of the commonly used and simplified word loibon, pl. loibons.

in the colonies. These German colonial companies could not prevail against the resistance of the local population, so the imperial government gradually usurped actual rule, and thus the "protectorates" became colonies. In the German colonies in German East Africa, the term "*Schutztruppe*" was used. The troops of the "*Schutztruppe*" were composed of German officers, medical and veterinary officers, non-commissioned officers, and civil servants who left the army for this job and transferred to the service of the *Schutztruppe* with the option to return. The troops in East Africa were initially filled by mercenaries from Sudan and Mozambique, and later throughout by enlisted locals called "Askari".

The *Schutztruppe* in German East Africa was occasionally supplemented by native auxiliaries, the so-called (in Kiswahili) "Rugaruga". They feared militias in the wake of the "*Schutztruppe.*" In colonial times, Rugaruga also referred to irregular auxiliaries provided by village communities or chiefs to the colonial forces on a case-by-case basis. Unlike the Askaris, Rugaruga were not part of regular colonial armies such as the German *Schutztruppe*. To identify themselves, they wore uniform parts or merely colored ribbons and patches.

2.4 German colonizers, traders, and settlers in East Africa

To better understand the political context and power relations of the time, one must look at the German colonization of Africa. At the beginning of the last quarter of the 19th century, the unified German Empire had emerged as a major world power and as the number three of empires ruling over "colonies." In 1885, right after the Berlin Conference, gunboats were dispatched to East Africa to contest the Sultan of Zanzibar's claims of sovereignty over the mainland in what is today Tanzania. The colony was officially established in an area already inhabited by a few German missionaries and merchants. Tanganyika was the largest of six countries that constituted Germany's African presence in the age of New Imperialism. The focus of the colonization was the economic exploitation of the soil and the people. Focusing on our case-study, I state: Mount Meru in north-eastern Tanzania has long been such a contested area, and struggles over land on the fertile, well-watered southern slopes of the mountain have featured strongly in its recent history. During the early nineteenth century, land was plentiful, and Arusha and Meru settlers expanded rapidly up its slopes. By the end of the century, Meru and Arusha had reached the upper limits of cultivation and came increasingly into conflict with one another, fighting over vacant areas between them (Spear, 1996).

2.5 The German imperial government at the center of Berlin

The importance of the imperial government of the extremely hierarchical German Empire of 1871 became visible at the "Berlin-Congo-conference" (1884/85). This event, also called the "Congress of Berlin", took place at the invitation of Otto von Bismarck (1815–1888), the imperial chancellor of the German Empire. This is how the mission-friendly words spoken by Bismarck as the Imperial Chancellor (1871–1899) on the 11th of December 1894 in the *Reichstag* went: "The government will least of all renounce the support of the Christian missionary societies, without whose sacrificial and beneficial activity, the entire colonial work would be called into question. The Government, for its part, will encourage the mission in every way, and give it full freedom in the exercise of its profession in all protectorates" (Paul, 1898: 20f, transl. M.F.).

2.6 German imperial government represented at the "margins" in East-Africa

Here I list some remarkable political decisions made by the German Empire. Their consequences go directly with entanglements and disentanglements, with foundations and conflicts within the framework of indigenous populations, between the Leipzig Mission Society and German colonial power from 1892 to 1904:

1884: Start of the territorial acquisitions of the *"Gesellschaft für Deutsche Kolonisation"* by Carl Peters in East Africa.

1884/85: Berlin-Congo Conference ("Scramble for Africa") coinciding with Germany's emergence as an imperial power.

1888: Treaty with the Sultan of Zanzibar: leasing of the coast to the *Deutsch-Ost-Afrikanische Gesellschaft*/D.O.A.G. (coast remains property of the Sultan).

1890: Heligoland-Zanzibar Treaty between the German and British empires.

1890: Government treaty with D.O.A.G. Takeover of the protectorate by the German Empire.

1890: The first Western settlers arrive at Mount Meru, cultivating and trading.

1891: *"Schutztruppe"* (imperial protection force) for German East Africa is established.

1892: Leipzig Mission's interest in work in East Africa matured: taking over the previous work of the Hersbruck Mission.

1895: Decree of colonial rulers published: land now belongs to the crown; natives of Kilimanjaro and Meru are confined to the upper slopes.

1896: Missionaries Ovir and Segebrock, although close to Captain Johannes, were killed during an attack by Arusha-warriors.

1896: Only some days after the "event" of October 20, the punitive expedition or massacre led by Captain Kurt Johannes together with Lieutenant Moritz Merker and 6000 Chagga auxiliaries against the Arusha and Meru.

1897: Introduction of a house and cottage tax for German East Africa.

1897/98: Arusha defeated after several punitive expeditions by Captain Johannes, one hundred deaths, destruction, rapes, and raids.

1900: Foundation of the military post (Boma) of Arusha by forced labor with Arusha-warriors (followed by the development of the village of Arusha).

1902: Leipzig's foundation of the mission-station Nkoaranga as the first one at Meru.

1904: Arrival of the Leipzig missionaries Fokken and Luckin. Foundation of the mission-station Ilboru at Arusha.

2.7 Entangled missions: Leipzig Mission, Church Missionary Society (CMS), Holy Ghost Fathers, and the two protagonists of the "event"

Berlin III Missionary Society, also known as the Evangelical Missionary Society for East Africa (EMS), was the first to send Lutheran missionaries from Germany. Their first missionary station was opened at Dar-es-Salaam in 1887. The third mission society (after Berlin II) was the Leipzig Mission Society. This society entered the country in 1893 and opened its first station at Kidia, Old Moshi in the Kilimanjaro region. The Leipzig Mission was not the first mission agency in that field, but the second. The British Church Missionary Society (CMS) established a station at Moshi on the slopes of Mount Kilimanjaro in 1885. In 1895, Karl Segebrock and Ewald Ovir were sent to German East Africa "to expand the Lutheran work westwards. The work among the Chagga of Kilimanjaro was well underway, and the enlargement of the Lutheran work was timely. Moreover, with increased competition from the Catholic Holy Ghost Fathers, swift expansion was considered necessary. In October 1896, after receiving orders from the board in Leipzig, Ovir and Segebrock traveled to Mount Meru to prepare for the foundation of a station amid the Meru people inhabiting the southeastern slopes of the mountain.

What are the profiles of Segebrock and Ovir?

Karl Segebrock (1872–1896) was born in 1872 in Mitau in Kurland (Imperial Russia). Under the impression of a missionary's sermon during his school days, he decided to become a missionary himself. In 1889, he entered the Leipzig Mission Seminary and passed the final examination at Easter 1895. In 1895, he was seconded to the Chagga Mission in East Africa, with missionary Ewald Ovir. He landed in Mombasa in 1895 and reached Mamba on September 19, 1895, where he worked with missionary Gerhard Althaus. Segebrock joined missionary Fassmann in Moshi (Old Moshi, today Kidia) in 1896 to establish this station. On October 13, 1896, he left for Meru with Missionary Ovir, where they planned to establish the station in Akeri/Meru.

Ewald Ovir (1873–1896) was born in 1873 in Jaggowall in Estonia (then Imperial Russia). He attended the governorate grammar school in Reval from 1883 to 1890 and then became a tutor. Through a doctor, he came into contact with the overseas mission. In 1891, he entered the Leipzig Mission Seminary. He was ordained in Leipzig in June 1895, and on June 5, 1895, Ovir was seconded together with missionary Karl Segebrock to the Chagga Mission in German East Africa. He landed in Mombasa and arrived in Machame on September 21, 1895, where he worked together with missionary Emil Müller. He left for Meru on October 13, 1896, with missionary Segebrock, where they planned to establish a station in Akeri/Meru. In an optimistic letter to Missionary Emil Müller, Ovir reported the day before about a friendly reception by Mangi Matunda, the Meru Chief. Ovir also noted that the Holy Ghost Fathers had not preceded them, although they had already surveyed the region and built a provisional hut.[9]

---

9   Comp. Groop, 2007, With the Gospel to Maasailand: 41: According to Mission Inspector Martin Weishaupt the competition with the Catholics was a major point for the Leipzig Mission to found stations around Mount Meru (comp. Weishaupt, 1912, in: Evangelisch-Lutherisches Missionsblatt: 534)

The main historical source one relays is more or less a compilation of different sources by the missionaries Müller and Faßmann, only half a year after the event in March 1897. The German title *"Die Bluttaufe unserer Mission am Meru. Nach Briefen von Müller und Faßmann"* (in English, "Blood Baptism of our Mission at Meru. According to letters by Müller and Faßmann") published in the mission's magazine *"Evangelisch-Lutherisches Missionsblatt* (ELMB)" from 1897. It contains two articles that express the entanglements of colonial and missionary and of religious and political interests, which are seen as separated on the one hand and directly related to one another: "Blood-baptism of our mission at Meru…" and "Punitive expedition to the Meru …"

Is it not fascinating that people (Indigenous for that matter) are not baptized here, but rather the mission itself? What does this mean? Is it a legitimizing of the mission through deaths interpreted as 'sacrifice'? Does it open up a window into uneasiness about legitimacy? Page 13 shows photographs of bust images of the two, underpinned with the words: "… murdered on October 20, 1896, on Mt. Meru." Again, below there are placed two biblical quotations: "These have come out of great tribulation." (Revelation 7:14) and "And they have offered up their souls for the name of our Lord Jesus Christ" (Acts 15:26). From pages 14 to 15 of this report, I count six of the eight relevant factors and actors that I have identified. On pages 56–57, the entanglement of mission and colonial power (*Schutztruppe*) is evident in the article with the title, *"Die Strafexpedition nach dem Meru"*, where the "punitive expedition to the Meru" is described as a fully justified reaction.

2.8 German mission societies headquarters at Leipzig/German Empire

Carl Paul (1857–1927) was a German Evangelical Lutheran theologian, pastor, missiologist, and author. He was the influential director of the Leipzig Mission (1911–1923) and was considered a respected expert on colonial mission in Germany at the beginning of the 20th century. We take notice of him among other actors, even if he was in charge around 15 to 20 years after the "Akeri-event". We can understand the situation of high-noon of German imperialism better, if we notice how he strategically entangles mission and imperialism in a shameless way. Paul agrees that in official parlance, overseas possessions at that time were often referred to as "protectorates" which shall be much more appropriate than the term "colonies". He demands that the natives' rights be protected. He claims that the first African territories did not arise from violent conquests, but from treaties of protection with native rulers. "We, the powerful nation whose arm now reaches into the interior of Africa and to the islands of our opposite feet, and whose voice counts for something in the council of nations, owe such protection to the much-troubled peoples of Africa and the South Seas." Paul refers to the situation around 1900 in the region of Arusha and Kilimanjaro: "The predatory Maasai, who until recently made the border areas of German and English East Africa unsafe, also enjoy the worst reputation as cattle and human thieves" (comp. Paul, 1898: 9).

2.9 "Chart of Entanglements" between various factors/actors at certain places

Various factors/actors, discursively entangled with each other at certain places and at specific times, structure and invigorate a space of violence exercised against others or of being violated. At the discursive intersections of two intersecting points of the variables X/Y we navigate through a qualitative analysis. These factors and their actors are more or less strongly related to each other:

"Chart of Entanglements"

Various factors/actors, discursively entangled with each other at certain places and at specific times structure and invigorate a space of exercised violence against others or of being violated ●	1. Traditional African societies' leadership	2. Coastal colonial regime of the Sultanate of Zanzibar	3. German military forces ("Imperial Schutztruppe")	4. German colonizers, traders, and settlers in East Africa	5. German (British) imperial government at the center in Berlin	6. German imperial government represented at the margins in East-Africa	7. German mission societies stations around Kilimanjaro and Meru*	8. German mission societies headquarters at Leipzig/ German Empire
1. Traditional African societies' leadership	●		●					●
2. Coastal colonial regime of the Sultanate of Zanzibar								
3. German military forces ("Imperial Schutztruppe")								
4. German colonizers, traders, and settlers in East Africa						●		
5. German (British) imperial government at the center in Berlin		●						●
6. German imperial government represented at the margins in East-Africa	●							
7. German mission societies stations around Kilimanjaro and Meru*								●
8. German mission societies headquarters at Leipzig/German Empire							●	

* Leipzig, Anglican CMS, Catholic HGF

2.10 Possible entanglements between various factors/actors at certain places and times, structuring and invigorating a discursive space

Herewith, I introduce the epistemological value and practical application of the diagram with the 8 factors. Navigation through discourses facing the wounds, made visible by variations of the intersecting relationships (X/Y-axis). The "wounds" inflicted either directly or indirectly are indicated by underlining passages that give symbolic expression to the victims.

1. Traditional African societies' leadership: intersected by point 1: regional internal conflicts between Chagga and Arusha misused for revenge by the protection force (1896ff)
2. Coastal colonial regime of the Sultanate of Zanzibar: Intersected point 5: Sultan Hamoud fully dependent on the British Empire after the Heligoland-Zanzibar-Treaty (1890)
    German military forces ("Imperial *Schutztruppe*"): Intersected by 1: Missing experience of living in foreign environments, lack of knowledge, permanent fear of attacks (1896)
3. German colonizers, traders, and settlers in East Africa: Intersected by 6: Confiscation of traditional land, access reserved to colonists, declared by the German government (1895)
4. German imperial government at the center in Berlin: Intersected by point 8: Government giving the mission freedom to exercise its profession in protectorates reveals the dependency of the mission on the state and the supposed imperial character of such a hegemonic "mission" (1884)
5. Imperial government represented in East-Africa: Intersected by point 1: Forced labor of Arusha-warriors, constructing the Boma of Arusha as collective punishment (1900)
6. German mission societies stations around Kilimanjaro and Meru (Leipzig, Anglican CMS, Catholic HGF): Intersected by point 8: Dependency: decisions like the foundation of a new station must be permitted by LM headquarters (1896)
7. German mission societies headquarters at Leipzig/German Empire: Intersecting point 1 and point 7: Wrong, tendentious information about the traditional religions, demonizing them, and reported by Leipzig missionaries as "objective truth" to Leipzig society's headquarters and the seminary may result in misunderstandings of the supposed superior missiologists.

3. Entangling vulnerability between various frontiers

At the end of these observations, let us remember the proposed research objectives. We wanted to

1. ... deconstruct and even re-construct the contextual situation of Segebrock and Ovir towards the various actors on the night of October 19 and 20, 1896 (Altena, 2003: 282-284).
2. ... find out the main motives of the involved German politicians as well as African actors in a process that resulted in the deaths of Segebrock and Ovir, referring to their self-understanding.
3. ... make visible the entanglements of power relationships between the Leipzig Mission and an African leadership stretched between resistance to missionary work and cooperation with it.

4. … define guidelines for a postcolonial understanding of the entangled history of mission at the interface of interrelated churches and Christians from the global "North" and "South."

3.1 A "wounded Mission": Who were the real "victims" at Mount Meru?

We owe the following quote to the Dutch theologian Eleonora Dorothea Hof, currently teaching and researching at the Researcher Center for Global Christianity and Mission, Boston University: "Vulnerability is, in this case, the openness, both towards the human other and towards the Divine."(Hof, 2016, 167) This statement may help us to understand more widely and deeply who may be designated as "victims" in an adequate ecumenical theological understanding of "witnessing to the Christian faith until death."[10]

3.2 The victims of the "Akeri killings" in the military contexts

I think we must understand the whole narrative of the event and its entanglements as a certain example of the tragic conquest of East Africa by the German Empire and its hegemonic interests. Akeri is a symbol of how Germans dehumanized Africans who were supposed to be subjects of the empire, stealing their dignity. Is that all? No! If we ask the Meru and Arusha Christians of today, Akeri is even a symbol for the resilience of the wounded Africans and a witness of their faith against terror and violence. "Faith" here means to accept this exceptional peace given by God and to gratefully receive the new life. The apostle Paul emphasizes that one can only obtain this new life as a gift from God, and not earn it through one's own performance.

3.3 The "Evangelical Calendar of Names" questioning a culture of remembrance

The Protestant Calendar of Names is a directory comparable to the Catholic Calendar of Saints, containing mainly personalities of the pre-Reformation period and of Protestantism. It was drafted in the first half of the 20th century under the auspices of the Evangelical Michael Brotherhood and officially released by the Council of the EKD in 1969. The Calendar of Names in its current form is included as an appendix in the Sunday and Holiday Calendar published by the Liturgical Conference of the Protestant Church in Germany.

"20 October: Karl Segebrock † and Ewald Ovir † 1896 Martyrs." The two names are in the calendar and designated with a small cross, which refers, according to the calendar's list of abbreviations, to "Blood Witness(es)", but not (sic!) "Martyrs" (Schulz, 1975: 2). In an oral tradition, Najabu, a Tanzanian co-worker, was with them and could hide during the event in the shrubs. He reports the very last words of Ovir addressing his murderers, "I die, but I thank you!"[11]

---

10 Riccardi, 2002, Salz der Erde, Licht der Welt. Glaubenszeugnis und Christenverfolgung im 20. Jahrhundert, Freiburg/Basel/Wien

11 In German: *„Ich sterbe, aber ich danke Euch!"*, reportet in: Müller/Faßmann, „Die Bluttaufe unserer Mission am Meru. Nach Briefen von Müller und Faßmann", in: Evangelisch-Lutherisches Missionsblatt (= ELMB), 1897: 12-19

Whether that witness is true or not (we cannot find that out anymore), we have to listen carefully to it, because it has already become a relevant element of the discourse. There is nothing about hate or revenge in it. Its narration by African churches in their history until today, e.g., the Evangelical Lutheran Church of Tanzania (ELCT), gives already a clear expression of their agreement to fundamental Christian ethics, contradicting an ius talionis.

The reaction of the defeated German "protection force" followed only after 11 days with the punitive expedition on October 31, 1896, the so-called "Rain War" – due to the extremely difficult weather conditions. Mattayo Kaaya, another person, a Meru who as a boy witnessed the event, reports the names of men and women who had been murdered and captured during the revenge of the Germans. I ask: Aren't these murdered people among them Arusha as well Meru, not also "blood-witnesses" of another kind?[12]

The grave at Akeri has to be understood as a place of remembrance and as a space, where religious and worldly, missionary and colonial interests culminate. In a postcolonial view, we can deconstruct the "Real." It is "not a narrative of events, but a series of symbolic systems." The photograph of the place of the event was taken on October 20, 1896, by Lieutenant Johannes, who made sure that the two murdered missionaries got buried. The place changed over the years, as various depictions in photographs show. From today's (last but not least social-anthropological) perspective, I ask, is it just a graveyard?" Isn't it more a "memorial" or a "mausoleum" or a religious "shrine" according to its use and purpose by the Christians of the Evangelical-Lutheran Meru Diocese? It would go beyond the scope of this paper to pursue this question further, but Akeri is, in my understanding, to be described as the open wound of the beginnings of Christianity in the region of Mount Meru, Tanzania. At least it is a place of remembrance. The plaque quotes Jacob 5:11 "Behold, we call blessed those who have endured." It is kept as a symbol of the need for reconciliation among a defeated humanity on all sides, including Germans as well as Africans of that region, colonizers as well as colonized, representing a humanity that ought to know that there is no victory except that of Christ.

3.4 Concluding remarks, beyond wounding entanglements in the war machine

It is wrong to call Ovir and Segebrock "martyrs"[13] for at least three reasons:
1. This term shouldn't theologically be used in a Christian-Protestant view due to its Roman-Catholic dogmatic understanding, as if bloodshed as a means of grace could substitute for human sin.

---

12 Comp. Klaus Peter Kiesel: „Kitabu cha Matthayo Kaaya", (the book of Mattayo Kaaya) no date/place, (archive Moshi).

13 Simon Parisius has shown in his BA-Thesis ("125 years of contested memory. A Discourse Analysis of the Reception of the Killing of two Leipzig Missionaries from a Postcolonial Perspective", Hermannsburg, 2021), how the use of the terminology was conceptionalized, politicized, and published right some months after the event by the Leipzig Missions director Carl von Schwartz himself and how this was just the start and the part of an extremely effective missionary discourse. Comp. Altena, 2003, "Ein Häuflein Christen mitten in der Heidenwelt des dunklen Erdteils": Zum Selbst- und Fremdverständnis protestantischer Missionare im kolonialen Afrika 1884-1918, Münster e.a.: 284 with footnote 460

Historically, the missionaries didn't die because of their faith but because they were seen as colonial invaders in alliance with the *"Schutztruppe"* in an extremely naive and miserably organized action of both actors, missionary and colonial.

Their blood was shed because their lives had been "squeezed" between the fronts of two armies (Arusha-Maasai in defense and *Schutztruppe* in aggression), which collided.

Finally, one almost has to ask, isn't it a "miracle" that 125 years of this discourse have led to so many self-confident Christian communities between Kilimanjaro and Meru? Is this (in an entangled-historical view) because of these first missionary attempts, or (in a transcendental-theological perspective) not rather because our faith is founded beyond these discouraging entanglements?

References

Arendt, Hannah (1986) Elemente und Ursprünge totalitärer Herrschaft. I. Antisemitismus. II. Imperialismus. III. Totale Herrschaft (Original engl. 1951). München: R. Piper

Altena, Thorsten (2003) „Ein Häuflein Christen mitten in der Heidenwelt des dunklen Erdteils". Zum Selbst- und Fremdverständnis protestantischer Missionare im kolonialen Afrika 1884-1918. Münster: Waxmann

Balandier, Georges (1970) Die koloniale Situation: ein theoretischer Ansatz. In: Albertini, R.v. (ed.), Moderne Kolonialgeschichte, Köln / Berlin: Kiepenheuer & Witsch, 105-124

Conrad, Sebastian/Shalini Randeria (2013) Einleitung: Geteilte Geschichten – Europa in einer postkolonialen Welt. In: Conrad, S. / Randeria, S. / Römhild, R. (eds.), Jenseits des Eurozentrismus. Postkoloniale Perspektiven in den Geschichts- und Kulturwissenschaften, Frankfurt a.M. / New York: Campus Verlag, 32-70

Fosbrooke, H.A. (1948) An Administrative Survey of the Masai Social System. In: Elliott, H.F.I. (ed.). Tanganyika Notes and Records 26. Dar es Salaam, 1-83.

Groop, Kim (2006) With the Gospel to Maasailand. Lutheran Mission Work among the Arusha and Maasai in Northern Tanzania 1904-1973, Abo: Oy Tibo-trading Ab

Hof, Eleonora Dorothea (2016) Reimagining Mission in the Postcolonial Condition. A Theology of Vulnerability and Vocation at the Margins, Zoetermeer: Amsterdam University Press.

Miller, P.A. (1999) Toward a Post-Foucauldian History of Discursive Practices. Configurations. 7/2, 227-246

Parsalaw, Jospeh Wilson (1999) A History of the Church, Diocese in the Arusha Region from 1904 to 1958. Erlangen: Erlanger Verlag

Ratschiller, Linda / Wetjen, Karolin, (2018) Verflochtene Mission. Ansätze, Methoden und Fragestellungen einer neuen Missionsgeschichte. In: Ratschiller, L. / Wetjen, K., (eds.). Verflochtene Missionen. Perspektiven auf eine neue Missionsgeschichte, Köln et al.: Böhlau Verlag, 9-25

Sarasin, Philipp (2011) Diskurstheorie und Geschichtswissenschaft. In: Keller, R., Hirseland, A., Schneider, W., Viehöver, W. (eds.). Handbuch Sozialwissenschaftliche Diskursanalyse. Band 1: Theorien und Methoden. Wiesbaden: Verlag für Sozialwissenschaften, 61-89

Schulz, Frieder (1975) Das Gedächtnis der Zeugen – Vorgeschichte, Gestaltung und Bedeutung des Evangelischen Namenkalenders, Göttingen: Vandenhoek & Rupprecht

Spear, Thomas (1996) Struggles for the Land. The Politics & Moral Economies of Land on Mount Meru, in: Maddox, G. / Giblin, J.L. / Kimambo, I.N. (eds.). Custodians of the Land. Ecology & Culture in the History of Tanzania, London: James Currey, 213-240

Spear, Thomas (1997) Mountain Farmers. Moral Economies of Land & Agricultural Development in Arusha & Meru, Oxford / Berkley & Los Angeles / Dar es Salaam: Mkuki na Nyota

Werner, Michael / Zimmermann, Bénédicte (2006) Beyond Comparison: Histoire Croisée and the Challenge of Reflexivity, in: History and Theory 45, 30-51

Emmanuel Majola

Geographical and Chronological Perspectives of Leipzig Missionaries' Activities, Around Meru land 125 years ago

"You are witnesses of these things" Lk. 24:48

The journey of witnessing the Word of Christ by Rev. Ewald Ovir and Rev. Karl Segebrock from the Leipzig Mission in Germany to Meru land ceased approximately 125 years ago. Their lives ended in Akeri village on October 20, 1896. This history can be read in every aspect of people's lives to date. Their physical graves still exist at Akeri. The spiritual and socioeconomic lives reveal the values of the bloodshed by missionaries. As South African Bishop Desmond Tutu said:

> *"Indeed, the blood of the martyrs, both black and white, proved once more to be the seed of the Church even here in Africa. Praise be to God for all his servants past and present who have given of themselves unstintingly for the sake of the Gospel." (cited by Parsalaw, 1999: 27)*

During the 19th century, it was impossible to separate colonial powers from missionaries' exploration activities and traditional African societies' leadership. It was through the Berlin Conference in 1884 that the door for Leipzig Mission activities in East Africa was opened. The safe journey of missionaries was guaranteed by governors or other colonial leaders. It was the same for Rev. Ewald Ovir and Rev. Karl Segebrock. During their visit, the governor of Tanganyika was Hermann von Wissmann (April 1895 – December 1896), and the head of Moshi Boma was Captain Kurt Johannes. He was the one who ensured the safe journey of Ewald Ovir and Karl Segebrock from Machame to Meru land.[14]

After mastering the Kimachame language, Ovir and Segebrock left Machame for Meru and Arusha, accompanied by porters from Kilimanjaro. They traveled with the permission and instructions of Captain Johannes from Moshi Boma.

On October 15, 1896, they arrived at Meru (Akeri village) as guests of honor of Chief Matunda of Meru land. They stayed safely for about five days, as stated by Parsalaw:

> *"On the 17th of Oct., 1896, the Wamachame porters arrived from Meru with a letter dated 15th, written by Missionary Ovir, informing brother Muller of their safe arrival and honorable reception they received from Mangi Matunda and his people." (ibid: 69)*

There was no danger for the missionaries to visit and stay peacefully at Akeri from October 15-18. The situation changed completely after the arrival of Captain Johannes and his wife Emily, accompanied by Lieutenant Moritz Merker and several guards, three days later. They pitched their camp about 1000 meters from the camp of Ovir and Segebrock. The situation became more complicated for two reasons. First, the survey of the mission plot was made by Captain Johannes camp and Chief Matunda, without involving the missionaries camp. Further work by Parsalaw (1999):

---

14 General Notes No. 140. Tanganyika Territory Gazette, 31.01.1931

"On the following day, the 19th of Oct., 1896, the plot of land was surveyed in the presence of Captain Johannes and payment of 25 Gora (bundles of calico cloth) was made. All negotiations were done in the camp of Captain Johannes and not in the camp of the Leipzig missionaries." (ibid: 69).

The second reason that caused a red alarm was the weapons handed over to the missionaries by Captain Johannes for their protection. It was not the need of the missionaries, but Captain Johannes decided to give them guns and ammunition for self-defense. Further work by Parsalaw (1999):

"Repeatedly they assured Captain Johannes that they were not at all in need of his protection as Johannes wanted them to spend the night in his Camp. Nevertheless Captain Johannes gave them some guns and ammunition for self-defense if the need arose". (ibid: 69).

Chief Matunda and the people surrounding the area heard rumors about a plan to attack the Wazungu. Mangi Matunda himself reported them to Captain Johannes. Captain Johannes neglected the information, assuming that the chief was drunk. Even the chiefs from Arusha brought the same information. At last, all three chiefs tried to convince Captain Johannes, but without success. Further work by Parsalaw (1999) supports this claim:

"Towards midnight, Mangi Matunda went to inform Captain Johannes in his Camp that the Ilarusa warriors really had a plan on that night to attack them. Captain Johannes did not take his report seriously because Mangi Matunda, as he brought the news of the attack was in a intoxicated as a result of too much consumption of pombe (beer). Mangi Matunda himself was informed by an Arusha woman who was also said to be already gone. At nine on the same night, the watchmen in the captain Johannes' camp reported to Captain Johannes that Rapaito and Massinde confirmed about the truth of the rumors of the attack and went to Mangi Matunda's homestead on that very night. At 3:15 on the same night, all three chiefs returned to Captain Johannes camp and Rapaito admitted to having seen three Ilarusa warriors not far from there, infact at Balbal-Sea (Lake Duluti near Tengeru)." (ibid: 71)

The rumors turned into reality when both camps were surrounded by Ilarusa warriors fighting with askaries. Further work by Parsalaw:

"At the moment Captain Johannes' own camp encircled by Ilarusa warriors and they overpowered his small band of Askaris who simply fired aimlessly to keep the attackers away and eventually managed to prevent them from carrying out their assault." (ibid: 72)

Captain Johannes' Askaris managed to protect him from the Ilarusa warriors, but not the missionaries. Therefore, the missionaries' camp, without Askaris, was attacked.

1. The Killings of Two Missionaries; October 20, 1896

From the above situation, on the night of the attack, it is clear that the two missionaries Ovir and Segebrock were killed due to a lack of or insufficient security. Further work by Parsalaw supports this claim: "What was heard next from the camp of the two missionaries was only one shot and howling and smashing of boxes, tins and bags followed." (ibid: 72).

Therefore, the fight between Captain Johannes and the Ilarusa warriors ended with the deaths of missionaries Ovir and Segebrock and other helpers of the missionaries.

When commemorating the 125th jubilee of the deaths of the missionaries at Akeri, it is now clear and must be taken seriously in the records that the missionaries were killed by Ilarusa and not Meru warriors. Thanks be to God for revealing the truth through the excellent writing of Joseph Parsalaw in his book: A History of the Church, Diocese in the Arusha Region from 1904 to 1958; wrote:

> *"The killings of missionaries Ovir and Segebrock were done by spears of Ilarusa warriors. Therefore, any assertion that it were Waro (Meru) warriors who killed the two pioneer missionaries is not the real truth." (ibid: 72).*

Early in the morning (October 20, 1896), Captain Johannes and his soldiers buried the bodies of the two missionaries and left for Moshi. The bodies of the Africans were left to be buried by Chief Matunda. During that time, the deceased body was to be brought to the bush, far from homes.

The Akeri killings revealed the long-standing grievances of Ilarusa against Captain Johannes and Lieutenant Moritz Merker. This shows that the Ilarusa warriors had a long plan to take revenge against the German colonialists. Further work by Parsalaw (1999) supports this claim:

> *"Later, Captain Johannes asserted that the Akeri killings were mainly due to the fear of the Ilarusa warriors to be forced to work for Europeans. This remained the reason for the killings of missionaries Ovir and Segebrock without mentioning the brutal punishment of flogging the Ilarusa warriors in October 1895, as reason for the killings of missionaries Ovir and Segebrock without mentioning the brutal punishment of flogging the Ilarusa warriors in October 1895 as it was formerly reported by Missionary Emil Müller" (ibid: 73).*

The report of the deaths of Ovir and Segebrock arrived at Machame to Rev. Müller on October 21, 1896, and he wrote a letter to the Leipzig Mission office mentioning the following:

a) The mission work in Meru land has been suspended, but we have the plot blessed with the blood of our brothers.

b) Let us pray to God to bring the Gospel of Christ to Meru inland in due time.

2. The Entanglement of Missionaries' Activities and Colonial Powers

Later, Captain Johannes returned to Arusha and destroyed many lives. Morani were killed, and animals such as cows, sheep, and goats were taken to Kware village in the Kilimanjaro region.

This is the evidence that shows the missionaries' journey and activities entangled with the colonial powers: the Coastal Colonial Regime of the Sultanate of Zanzibar, German military forces, German colonizers, traders, and settlers in East Africa as well as African traditional leaders. All those powers come together to attack Arusha - Meru

> *"On the 31st of October, 1897, ten days after the assault in Akeri, Captain Johannes together with Lieutenant Merker, Dr. Eggel, 100 Askaris, and thousands of excited Wachagga warriors led by Mangi Shangali and Meli started off to Arusha." (ibid: 78)*

On the other hand, it can be compared with the portrayal of the Ujamaa policy during the 1970s-80s. The church, especially the Lutheran, entangled (agreed) with the government self-reliance and Ujamaa policy (Maanga, 2012: 47).

3. Second Leipzig Missionary Journey in February 1902

After six years (1896–1902), the missionaries' activities reached Meru land for the second time and settled at Nkoaranga. On June 18, 1905, eleven people were baptized at the Nkoaranga Mission Center. The first baptism marked a remarkable event in the Meru Lutheran Church.

The seed of the blood of two missionaries, Ovir and Segebrock, reveals the power of the Word of God. Jesus Christ answered the prayers of Rev. Müller and brought back the gospel to Meru inland in due time. The missionary core activities were preaching and baptizing Meru people, educating people in co-education, and providing and giving people medical care.

The Gospel of Jesus Christ was brought back to Meru land after the arrival of Rev. Arno Krause and Kurt Fickert on February 24, 1902. They arrived in Tanganyika during the reign of Governor Gustav Adolf von Gotzer (March 12, 1901 – April 15, 1906).

The missionaries visited Chief Nyereu at Mbembe-Nkoaranga village. A house had already been constructed under the orders of Lieutenant Wilhelm Merker, the successor of Captain Johannes. The installation of chief Nyereu and the construction of a guest house at Mbembe, even before the arrival of the missionaries, is an indication of the colonial power behind the missionaries' activities.

The missionaries and their delegation asked the chief's permission to teach the people God's word. The Chief and his family welcomed them, and the following day, February 25, 1902, the Chief gave them the area near the Mbembe River. Immediately, teaching activities started in April. The first Sunday service was held on May 2, 1902. Around May 1902, two core activities began: preaching the Gospel of Jesus Christ and teaching people to read and write.

125 years later, the Lutheran Church celebrates the tremendous development in Meru land. Nobody can deny the progress made by missionaries' activities, which pioneered development in all aspects of people's lives in Meru land. This development of the church must go in parallel with that of the Meru local government.

4. The Growth of Missionary Activities

Geographical and chronological perspectives for about 125 years ago, in Meru land, witnessed the socioeconomic and geographical changes broadly within and outside the Church. Preaching the Gospel of Jesus Christ, teaching people co-education, and offering medical care proved progress beyond the Akeri killing and the revenge.

4.1. Growth of the Church

From the start of the missionary center at Nkoaranga (February 24, 1902) through the first baptism on June 18, 1905, Meru land became one of the districts of the Northern Diocese in

1972. After 20 years, on June 21, 1992, Meru District became an autonomous Diocese of the Evangelical Lutheran Church in Tanzania (ELCT – DME).

From the first eleven new convents in the Meru area at Nkoaranga to date, teaching and preaching of the gospel and growth of the church members have reached the tremendous numbers of 159 congregations (preaching points), 59 parishes, and five districts. Today, the Diocese of Meru has a total of 78,144 church members and 96 pastors (73 in office and 23 retired). The pastors are assisted by 167 evangelists and 17 parish workers[1]. These pastors, evangelists, and parish workers serve in different parishes, congregations, and other institutions within and outside the Diocese of Meru.

4.2. Education Services

Meru land which covers Meru District Council, is a region that runs many schools (pre- and primary), secondary schools, and colleges. In the Meru area, both government and private primary schools amount to 170 in total and are scattered in 26 wards of the Meru District Council. The government owns 115 primary schools. About 55 schools have a private ownership. Within the Meru area, there are 66 secondary schools, 37 owned by the government and 29 private. There are several vocational schools as well as colleges and universities.

All these teaching and learning centers bring awareness, education, perfection, and knowledge brightening the horizons of individuals and communities.

What matters most, is Christianity's spirit; thirst for education, and fight for physical development. Among the schools and colleges, the Diocese of Meru owns six secondary schools, two primary schools, and four vocational schools.

4.3. Medical Care

Since the first admission of eight patients to Nkoaranga dispensary (hospital) in May 1904, there have been five dispensaries, one health center, and Nkoaranga hospital owned by the church (Meru Diocese).[2]

4.4. Infrastructure

The road network is available throughout Meru land. It is possible to reach every village and sub-villages regardless of challenges during the rainy season. Hydro electricity supply has reached every ward and is fully supplied in many villages. Drinking water supply has been distributed, and many water projects are in process. The church, the Diocese of Meru, supported many water projects, such as the Akeri, Urisho, Ngarenanyuki, and King'ori to Malula water projects. Recently, the Diocese of Meru through donors, sup- ported the Kikwe-Maweni water project. The challenges are to be solved daily as a result of rapid population growth due to the rate of urbanization and the decline of water sources as a result climate change.

---

1   ELCT Meru Diocese Archives
2   ibid.

5. Conclusion

From the main core of missionary activities, the main purpose was the development of mankind, people's better lives, and a well-structured society. The incidence of attacks and Akeri killings was not planned by the indigenous people, but it was a way of taking revenge against colonial rulers. Further work by Parsalaw (1999) supports this claim:

> *"The Ilarusa and Meru warriors were in the land since the arrival of the two Leipzig Missionaries. They could have been killed on the first day of their arrival in Akeri or Kirengo if there was such a plan." (ibid: 70).*

Therefore, the Ilarusa warriors killed the Leipzig Missionaries because of the friction between the indigenous people and colonial power and not due to the coulor of missionaries.

From 1896 to date, the progress made by missionaries, now the Church, has been remarkable. The path through and the safety of missionaries under the colonial rulers enabled the implementation of core activities such as preaching the gospel, co-education, and health services. Regardless of the degree of revenge, the development of mankind in Meru land, now the Meru Diocese within the Meru District Council, is among the best areas in Tanzania.

During the celebration/anniversary of 125 years ago of the killings at Akeri, the growth of the Meru District Council and the Church (the Diocese of Meru), is overwhelming. We thank God that the deaths of the two missionaries, and the prayer of Rev. Muller and other missionaries opened the door for the second journey and spread of Christianity, as well as socioeconomic growth in Meru land and the ELCT Diocese of Meru in Meru District Council in general.

"For me, to live is Christ, and to die is gain." Flp. 1:21

References

Maanga, Godson S. (2013) Injili kamili: Historia ya kanisa la kiinjili la Kilutheri Tanzania 1963-2013. Moshi, New Millennium Books

Parsalaw, J.W. (1999) A History of the Church, Diocese in the Arusha Region from 1904 to 1958. Erlangen, Erlanger Verlag für Mission und Ökumene

Joseph W. Parsalaw

The Akeri Killings in 1896[1]

Before discussing the killings of missionaries Ovir and Segebrock in Akeri, let us examine the nature of relations that existed between the Ilarusa and the Wameru before the arrival of the German colonial government in the area. The Ilarusa were adopted by the Ilkisongo Masai and worked for them for years, providing their masters with produce from their small *shambas*. The Masai treated them as "Ilmeek" – a highly pejorative term applied to those who were not "pure" Masai. After their population had increased, the Ilarusa, tired of this ascribed inferiority, decided to free themselves once and for all. A decisive battle was fought in Kirako, near the small town of Engare-Olmotonyi (Merker, 1910: 20). The Masai were pushed far south, enabling the Ilarusa to occupy large adjacent grazing lands on the plains.

The defeat of the Masai gave Ilarusa control over neighbouring tribes, especially the Wameru. Gulliver says that around the year 1840, Ilarusa warriors of the Iltwati and Ilnyangusi age set raided the Wameru with increasing success, from time to time acquiring large numbers of Meru women and cattle. Women from Meru were adopted into Ilarusa families, circumcised, married, and incorporated into the appropriate age set of the Ilarusa as fellow Morani (warriors) (Gulliver, 1963: 33). Meru land is said to have reached the present Sokon area near the Temi River. Through their skillful war tactics, the Ilarusa managed to push the Wameru back from the border of the Temi River to the present border between Wameru and Ilarusa, which is the Nduruma River. The defeated Wameru warriors copied the Ilarusa mode of dress, hairstyle, and military tactics. They spoke the Ilarusa dialect of the Maa language.

In those days, the Wameru were under the control of the Ilarusa and forced to pay tribute to their masters. Missionary Ittameier, who for many years worked at Nkoaranga in Meru, reported that the Meru for many years before the coming of the Germans, were under the dominion of the Ilarusa and were obliged to pay tribute. The grandfather of Chief Matunda is said to have been the first chief of the Meru selected by them to collect the tribute demanded by the Ilarusa. The tribute that the Meru had to pay the Ilarusa was actually the reason for them to select a chief. "For a long time, the land of the Meru was subject to Arusha and had to pay tribute" (*Lange Zeit ist das Meruland Arusha unterworfen und tributpflichtig gewesen*) (ELMB, 1940: 56-72).[2] Therefore when the Germans occupied this part of East Africa, Meru land was in the hands of the Ilarusa, which explains the presence of Arusha men in Meru when the missionaries Karl Segebrock and Ewald Ovir arrived at the homestead of Matunda of Meru in 1896.

Missionary Emil Müller of Machame later attributed the tragic killing of Ovir and Segebrock in Akeri to corporal punishment inflicted upon the Ilarusa people by Captain Kurt Johannes, the Imperial Commissioner stationed in Moshi:

---

1   This contribution is based on a chapter in my dissertation, A History of the Lutheran Church Diocese in the Arusha Region from 1904 to 1958 (Erlangen, 1999)

2   ELMB = Evangelisch-Lutherisches Missionsblatt

"After Captain Johannes had punished the inhabitants of Arusha in October 1895, having raided the Meru people, we believed that peace and security prevailed now in Meru. That is why we let Brother Ovir move there at the beginning of August, so that he could negotiate with Matunda, the Chief of Meru land and with Rapaito, the influential chief from Arusha, about the construction of a mission station."[3]

In reality, however, Rapaito had never been a chief in any part of Arusha but was a military commander under Mangi Ndasikoi, close to the border with the Wameru. The presence of Rapaito in Meru land was due to the Arusha hegemony in Meru.[4] Missionary Müller's assumption that peace and security prevailed in Arusha after Captain Johannes and his native Askaris had punished the Ilarusa, is not convincing. On the contrary, after the punitive expedition against the Ilarusa the situation in Arusha became worse. The warriors of the land were instructed to be in a state of readiness against any surprise attack from the Germans residing in the vicinity of Kilimanjaro.

October 12, 1896, Mangi Shangali of Machame was requested to provide 60 porters to carry the luggage of missionaries Ovir and Segebrock to the land of Mangi Matunda of Meru the following day. Unable to provide the required number of porters and not wishing to antagonize the much-feared Captain Johannes, who was expected to arrive in Nkoarungo on the 14th, Shangali pleaded earnestly with Missionary Müller not to complain to Captain Johannes, assuring him that he would find more porters (Tagebuch der Missionsstation Madschame vom 11-13 Oct. 1896, Missionar Müller).

October 17, 1896, the Wamachame porters arrived from Meru with a letter dated October 15, written by Missionary Ovir, informing Brother Müller of their safe arrival and the respectable reception they had received from Mangi Matunda and his people. On the 18th, Captain Johannes and his wife Emily, accompanied by Lieutenant Moritz Merker and several Askaris, arrived in Akeri and pitched camp about 1000 meters from the camp of Ovir and Segebrock. Captain Johannes and his band were heading for Umbugwe, and he happened to stop in Akeri to greet the missionaries there (ibidem). On the following day, October 19, 1896, the plot of land was surveyed in the presence of Captain Johannes, and payment of 25 Gora (bundles of calico cloth) was made. All negotiations were done in the camp of Captain Johannes and not in that of the Leipzig missionaries. In the process of demarcating the plot of land and payment, "influential Arusha people", Rapaito and Masinde, were present (ibidem). Neither Missionary Müller nor Johannes explained in what sense these two men were "influential".

It will be noted that Ovir and Segebrock had been in the area for at least five days without any hatred or dislike being shown by the natives or by the "influential Arusha" people. Re-

---

3   *„Nachdem Herr Hauptmann Johannes die Bewohner von Aruscha im Oktober 1895 dafür gezüchtigt hatte, daß sie die Meru Leute überfallen hatten, glaubten wir, daß am Meru nun Friede und Sicherheit herrsche und ließen deshalb Br. Ovir Anfang August unbedenklich dorthin ziehen, damit er mit Matunda, dem Häuptling der Landschaft Meru und mit Rawaito, dem einflußreichsten Häuptling von Arusha wegen der Anlage einer Station verhandele."*

4   *„Die Waro waren vor der europäischen Herrschaft Knechte der Aruschaleute. Jetzt sind sie frei, sie ahmen die Sitten der Aruschaleute nach und verstehen auch vielfach ihre Sprache, das Masai. Aber noch heute haben sie eine starke Abneigung gegen ihre einstigen Herren."* Missionary Leonard Blumer, Evangelisch-Lutherisches Missionsblatt, 1925: 13

peatedly, they assured Captain Johannes, who wanted them to spend the night in his camp, that they were not in need of his protection (Müller, 1936: 16).[5] Nevertheless, Johannes gave them some guns and ammunition for self-defence, should the need arise. Captain Johannes himself reported afterward to his superiors in Dar es Salaam:

> *"I gave the gentlemen a few guns and some ammunition, not for their sake but because it is easy for a fight to break out all of a sudden among the people and that it is better if they have something in their hands."[6]*

The next news to reach Missionary Müller in Machame was a brief note of condolence written by Johannes, informing him about the deaths of missionaries Ovir and Segebrock, which occurred on the night of October 19th–20th 1896 (ELMB, 1897: 12-19). Ilarusa warriors were reported to be responsible for the deaths of the two missionaries. Ilarusa and Meru warriors had been in the land since the arrival of the two Leipzig missionaries. They could have been killed on the day of their arrival in Akeri if there had been a plan. I am therefore inclined to believe that the arrival of Captain Johannes must have aroused the suspicion of the "influential" Arusha people present in Meru land. After seeing their enemy, Captain Johannes, interfering in the affairs of the missionaries, this close contact between the Wazungu (Europeans) must have led them to regard Ovir and Segebrock as spies sent ahead by Captain Johannes.

Assuming that Johannes and his Askaris had not involved themselves in the affairs of Ovir and Segebrock, perhaps the Ilarusa warriors would in the course of time have learned to know the difference between Captain Johannes and the two missionaries. But the regimentation and the guns carried by both missionaries and Johannes implied no distinction at all between bringers of the Gospel and mercenaries. Captain Johannes in his report concerning the murder of the two missionaries said:

> *"On the evening of October 18, 1896, Chiefs Rapaito and Massinde, the influential chiefs from Arusha, arrived at my camp and denied knowing anything about the rumors of a war. On the 18th and 19th both missionaries were in my camp for several hours, or rather I with Lieutenant Merker was at their camp, where we discussed about the situation in Meru land and especially the rumors of unrest there. On the contrary, the gentlemen (Ovir and Segebrock) very much praised the reception they were accorded there in Meru and also mentioned the friendly approach of the natives, whereby they brought daily foodstuffs to sell to them there at their camp. Upon my request for them to stay in my Camp just in case, and later to return to their station, the gentlemen replied that there existed absolutely no danger whatsoever to their lives."[7]*

---

5   See also the official report, "Amtlicher Bericht über die Ermordung der zwei Missionare Ovir und Segebrock in Akeri. Der kaiserliche Stationschef gez. Johannes, Kompaniefuhrer, Moshi den 23. Oktober 1896" (in the possession of the author)

6   *„Ich habe den Herren ein paar Mausergewehre und Patronen mitgegeben, nicht ihretwegen, sondern weil es leicht mal unter den Leuten selber Raufereien geben kann, und da ist es schon besser, wenn sie etwas in Händen haben."*

7   *„… am 18. Oktober 1896 abends trafen die Häuptlinge Rawaito und Massinde, die einflußreichsten von Groß Arusha in meinem Lager und dementierten die Kriegsgerüchte. Am 18. und 19. waren die beiden Missionare mehrere Stunden in meinem Lager, oder ich mit Leutnant Merker bei ihnen, wo wir über die Verhältnisse am*

Therefore with a feeling of security the two missionaries slept in their camp.

Towards midnight, Mangi Matunda went to inform Captain Johannes in his camp that the Ilarusa warriors had a plan to attack them that night. Johannes did not take his report seriously, because Mangi Matunda was intoxicated as a result of consuming too much *pombe* (beer). Mangi Matunda had been informed by an Arusha woman, who had already departed. At nine on the same night, the watchmen in Captain Johannes' camp reported to Johannes that Rapaito and Massinde confirmed the truth of the rumors of the attack and had gone to Mangi Matunda's homestead. At 3:15, all three chiefs returned to Captain Johannes' camp, and Rapaito admitted having seen three Ilarusa warriors not far from there, at Lake Balbal (Lake Duluti, near Tengeru) (Amtlicher Bericht über die Ermordung der zwei Missionare Ovir und Segebrock in Akeri). At that moment, Captain Johannes' own camp was encircled by Ilarusa warriors, whose small band of Askaris fired aimlessly to keep the attackers away and eventually managed to drive them off. From the camp of the missionaries, people heard only one shot, followed by howling and the smashing of boxes, tins, and bags. At daybreak, Captain Johannes and Merker with their Askaris hurried to the camp of the missionaries and found the bodies of Ovir and Segebrock with over 30 spear stabs at the spot where their tent had stood. Beside the two missionaries lay the body of a Chagga boy, identified by a porter named Rajabu as Missionary Ovir's houseboy. Rajabu is said to have hidden himself and, by good luck, escaped death (ibidem).

On the night of the killings, the assault was directed against the two camps indiscriminately. It was only good luck that saved Captain Johannes, whose Askaris fired furiously to keep the approaching Ilarusa warriors away (ibidem). The killing of Ovir and Segebrock was done by the spears of Ilarusa warriors, not by Wameru. Having buried the two missionaries, Captain Johannes and Lieutenant Merker returned in a hurry to Moshi. The Ilarusa warriors pursued them and their small band of Askaris up to the banks of the Sanya or Kikavu River. Some Arusha people I asked as to why the Ilarusa warriors refrained from capturing Captain Johannes and his Askaris narrated to me that it was because of a European woman who aborted on the banks of the River Kikavu. Presumably, Johannes' wife took a bath on the bank of the River Kikavu. Being in a hurry, she may have left behind her playing puppet, which the Ilarusa warriors took to be a miscarriage, and out of compassion, the warriors decided to turn back. Klaus Peter Kiesel, who has worked for some years in Meru land as a missionary, has likewise heard this story of a puppet that saved Captain Johannes and his small band of Askaris.[8]

After the two missionaries were buried, rumor was spread that the Ilarusa warriors exhumed the bodies of the missionaries and sliced them into pieces. The only plausible explanation here is that if the grave was dug in a hurry, it was not deep enough to prevent wild animals from exhuming and devouring the bodies. In 1902, Missionary Krause reported

---

Meru und besonders über die Nachrichten von eventuellen Unruhen sprachen. Sehr lobend sprachen sich die Herren über die Aufnahme aus, die sie dort gefunden hatten und über das freundliche Entgegenkommen der Eingeborenen, die ihnen täglich reichlich Lebensmittel zum Verkauf in ihr Lager brachten. Auf meine Aufforderung, doch für alle Fälle in mein Lager zu kommen und eventuell wieder auf ihre früheren Stationen zurück zu kehren, erwiderten die Herren, daß für ihr Leben absolut gar keine Gefahr bestehe."

8   Interview with Mchungaji missionary Klaus Peter Kiesel at Neuendettelsau, July 20, 1995

to Leipzig that after digging out the grave about two meters, he found no more bones and thought that the bodies must have been dug up and cut into pieces. My informants never mentioned such an action (ELMB, 1902: 282).

Later, Captain Johannes asserted that the Akeri killings were mainly due to the fear of the Ilarusa warriors of being forced to work for the Europeans (ELMB, 1897: 16).[9] He did not mention the brutal flogging of the Ilarusa warriors in October 1895, as reported by missionary Emil Müller (Ibid, 12). Müller reviewed what he believed to have been the cause of the Akeri killings in his booklet "Blutzeugen am Meru" (Blood Witnesses at Meru), published on the occasion of the 100th anniversary of the Leipzig Mission in 1936. Here he claimed:

> *"... many possible causes and reasons, but perhaps only one: God's appointed time for the Meru people had not yet come. That there could also be Europeans different from officers and officials was in fact noticed by the Meru people, but that others could also be servants of God was, for them, in that short time until 1896, only heard with their ears. But with understanding and heart, they did not grasp it at all. For them, missionaries Segebrock and Ovir were simply 'Wazungu' or Europeans, just like all other Europeans. And while the missionary in Africa was thought never to be in danger, they were recognized as warriors and therefore attacked by other warriors, fought, and were killed, indeed as warriors, whom one had learned to defeat. As murderers, these ancient pagans from Meru came to be conscious of their deeds later. We do not want to think only as Christians and friends of the mission work but also as Europeans with a broader and a deeper view; since our own ancestors had similar deeds and ideas. Pagans can only think and act as pagans." (Müller, 1936: 18-19)[10]*

That became the new version of the claim that the warriors were not aware in 1896 that there were different kinds of Wazungu. This is because, in speech and appearance, Ovir and Segebrock resembled the other German military men. Furthermore, the killers of the two missionaries never knew the different functions between missionaries and German soldiers. All of them carried guns, even if only for self-protection. Therefore, missionary Müller concluded that Ovir and Segebrock were perceived as German soldiers and hence killed (ibi-

---

9   He wrote to the Mission Director on October 31, 1896: *„Die Veranlassung zu dem mörderischen Anfall scheint, so viel bisher bekannt, darin zu suchen zu sein, daß die Leute sich der Niederlassung von Europäern in ihren Landschaften widersetzen wollten, in der Furcht, dann zur Arbeit herangezogen zu werden."*

10   *"... viele mögliche Ursachen und Gründe, vielleicht aber nur die eine: Gottes Zeit für den Meru war noch nicht gekommen. Daß es auch andere Europäer geben könne als Offiziere und Beamte, war von den Meruleuten zwar auch schon beobachtet worden, daß manche aber auch Diener Gottes und damit seine Boten an ein Volk sein könnten, war in der kurzen Zeit bis 1896 von ihnen nur mit den Ohren gehört, aber mit Verstand und Herz überhaupt nicht begriffen worden. So waren ihnen die Missionare Segebrock und Ovir 'Wazungu', Europäer, wie alle andern, und während sonst der Missionar in Ostafrika so gut wie unverletzlich war, wurden sie als Krieger von Kriegern angegriffen, bekämpft und getötet, ja auch hernach noch als Krieger, die man endlich einmal 'besiegen' gelernt hatte, angesehen. Als Mord ist diesen Urheiden vom Meru ihre Tat erst später zum Bewußtsein gekommen. Daran wollen wir nicht nur als Christen und Missionsfreunde, sondern auch als Europäer mit weiterem und tieferem Blick denken; denn unsre eignen Vorfahren haben bei ähnlichen Taten auch ähnliche Gedanken gehabt. Heiden können eben auch nur als Heiden denken und handeln."*

dem).[11]

Vengeance for the Deaths of Ovir and Segebrock

In vengeance for the deaths of the above-mentioned missionaries, Captain Johannes decided to conduct a punitive expedition against the Ilarusa. Regarding the deaths of the two Europeans as a challenge to his position, he planned to inflict punishment, which the Ilarusa would live to tell their grandchildren. To start with, "Rapaito", described by Missionary Müller as an "influential Arusha man", was killed. Müller, who was then at Nkoarungo Mission Station, reported:

> *"In the afternoon on the day before the march into Arusha, Chief Rapaito from Arusha came into [Captain Johannes'] camp ostensibly to greet him, but in reality to try to spy. It subsequently became obvious that he had played fast and loose. After the killings, the loot was divided at his place, and that is why the warriors of the expedition seized him near the camp on their way home and cut his throat." (ELMB, 1897: 52)[12]*

Arusha elders tell until today the story of how Rapaito was brutally killed upon the orders of Captain Johannes. Rapaito was one of the best spokesmen (Olaiguanani) and warriors of the Ilarusa. He belonged to the Iltalalani age set, whose members were promoted to senior warriors in about 1906, the same year as the commencement of the initiation of the Iltwati age set (Gulliver, 1963: 33). According to information obtained from Lemburis Abel Ole Sirikwa, the age set of Iltalalani and the not yet initiated Iltwati were the ones who fought the Germans. Rapaito was not a chief, as most reports claim. He was one of the four commanders of Mangi Ndasikoi Naparan'g, son of Oloolbela, who ruled the area east of Arusha on the Meru border.[13]

The assault in Akeri was planned by Mangi Ndasikoi Naparan'g and led by his war commanders Raito, Meraai, Makaine and Olmeeng'ienga. Olkarsis Simeon Bene ole Kokan, who was among the first generation of Ilarusa Christians, reported about this assault when he was ninety-three:

> *"I was about eight when I witnessed the first battle between the Germans and Masai. It was a black page in our history. Our people were forced to submit to the arrogance of the Germans. They flogged four of our field commanders, then hanged them in public because they resisted German entry into Arusha. Fortunately, we had a fearless commander, Ol-Meengi'enga, 'the ever-fighting', a man of unyielding will. His code name in battle was Ole Darpoy, 'sausage tree', referring to the endless stamina contained in a slender, tall frame. The Germans did not capture him. He lived to be one hundred." (Saibull/Carr, 1981: 115)*

Olmeegi'enga escaped death by hanging, as Mangi Ndasikoi was summoned to appear in

---

11   See also Anton Nelson, The Freemen of Meru, London, New York, 1967, 9-11
12   *„Am Nachmittag vor dem Einmarsch in Arusha kam der Häuptling Rawaito von Arusha ins Lager, angeblich zur Begrüßung, in Wahrheit zum Ausspionieren desselben. Es hat sich nachher gezeigt, daß er ein falsches Spiel getrieben hat. Bei ihm ist nach der Mordtat der Raub geteilt worden, deshalb haben Krieger der Expedition auf dem Rückwege in der Nähe des Lagers ihn ergriffen und ihm die Kehle durchgeschnitten."*
13   Lemburis A. Ole Sirikwa, letter to the author dated 3.5.1995

Moshi with his commanders. Ndasikoi was escorted by a troop of Ilarusa warriors to the Moshi Boma (fort), where he together and his troop were locked up. Ndasikoi remained in prison for some time and was then released together with his troop of Ilarusa warriors. Two of his commanders were jailed until 1900 when they, together with Mangi Meli of Moshi, were hanged. When Mangi Ndasikoi and his commanders were requested to appear in Moshi, Olmeengi'enga instead fled to Central Masai to a place called Engarenaibor, east of Longiito (Longido) in what is now Monduli District. He changed his old name Olmeengi'enga to a fake name, Ole Darpoy.[14]

Missionary Müller confirms Sirikwa's statement that "Masinde", meaning "Olmeengi'ebga, took refuge in Monduli"[15]: "One of the murderers was killed in the fight with several shots to his head; another fled. The other culprit, Mangi Masinde escaped to Monduli."

On October 31 1896, ten days after the assault in Akeri, Captain Johannes, together with Lieutenant Merker, Dr. Eggel, 100 Askaris and thousands of excited Wachagga warriors led by Mangi Shangali and Meli set off for Arusha.

The exact number of Chagga warriors who sided with Captain Johannes to fight the feared Ilarusa warriors is estimated to have been between 8 and 10,000.[16] Most of them were filled with impatience and excitement at the thought of looting their enemies. This was their chance to avenge the constant raids, oppression, and plunder to which the Ilarusa had subjected them in recent years. After putting up stiff resistance, the Ilarusa warriors under their able field commanders were defeated, and Captain Johannes became their new master (*bwana*). His Askaris went about the land, shooting and butchering whatever moved; the Ilarusa with their traditional war weapons, were helpless. Thousands ran away to seek safety in the forest, leaving behind their cattle. Houses and maize stored in trees were set on fire to make sure that those who ran away did not have food and shelter when they returned.

Missionary Müller reported that six hundred Ilarusa warriors were killed on the battlefield and hundreds were badly wounded.[17] The land was left in a state of ruin. This was the peace and order brought to the Ilarusa by the imperial commissioner, Captain Kurt Johannes. The number of cattle taken to Kilimanjaro was 10,000, and a great number of goats, sheep, and human beings were taken along with other booty. One of the Ilarusa captives taken to Kili-

---

14 Sirikwa, Ibidem

15 *„Einer der Mörder ist im Gefecht von mehreren Schüssen in den Kopf gefallen, ein anderer ist entflohen. Der andere schuldige Häuptling Masinde ist weit nach Mondule entkommen."* Diary of Müller, November 30, 1896. Captain Johannes in his own report said: *„Nachdem die Herren beerdigt waren und ich die vorgefundenen Sachen in leeren Kisten und Koffer hatte verpacken lassen, marschierte ich aus der Landschaft heraus. Sofort konnte ich strafend nicht eingreifen, da ich nur 50 Askari bei mir hatte und außerdem die Mörder bereits entflohen waren... Ich marschierte deshalb gleich nach Moschi zurück, einmal um nachdem ich mich der Teilnahme der Wadjagga an einer Strafexpedition gegen den Meru [= Arusha) vergewissert hatte, so schnell als möglich zu dieser aufbrechen zu können, andererseits aber auch in der Lage zu sein, die am Berg liegenden Missionsniederlassung zu schützen, [...] Aus diesem Grunde kann ich auch mit der Bestrafung nicht warten, bis eine eventuelle Unterstützung von der Küste hier eingetroffen ist. Ich marschiere deshalb am 31.d.M. mit 95 Askari und 2-3 Tausend Wadjagga als Hilfstruppen nach dem Meru-Berg ab."*

16 Ibidem

17 Ibidem

manjaro was Lodoku Sakala Rerei. He went to school in Mamba, was baptized there, and returned to Arusha in 1904, when Ilboru Mission Station was founded. He subsequently worked as a teacher at the Kimandolu outstation. From the loot, Mangi Shangali himself took 500 cattle. The Ilarusa were requested to pay tribute and surrender their weapons as a condition for what Johannes called peace.[18] Although Ilarusa warriors were well prepared to fight Captain Johannes, they were not successful because Johannes used the Chagga chiefs and their subjects to fight the Ilarusa. Had there been unity among these tribes, it would have been difficult for the small number of Askaris to defeat the Ilarusa. As Iliffe remarks:

> *"Because the inland people were disunited, the Germans were able to ally with one society against its neighbours, or to support one group within a society to the disadvantage of its competitors." (Iliffe, 1969: 12ff)*

It may perhaps not be wrong to blame the other Leipzig missionaries in Machame, Mamba and Moshi stations for simply keeping quiet. One point is clear: Ovir and Segebrock were neither in the service of the German colonial government nor under the supervision and protection of Captain Johannes. Perhaps the missionaries, hearing of the sudden death of their beloved colleagues, recalled how, more than 11 centuries earlier, Bonifatius (Boniface) was killed by German pagans. Tradition says that Boniface's followers would have defended him, but he told them: "Do not fight, for we are bidden to return good for evil. Be brave and have no fear of those who can kill only the body." (Bainton, 1950: 82)

Although Olmeengi'enga ran away to Monduli to save his life and changed his name, the blood of the missionaries whom he had killed haunted him. In 1962, Jesus Christ received him under the name Ole Darpoy to be one of many children. Rev. Maliaki M. Lukumay of the Monduli congregation, who was present at his baptism, reported that Ole Darpoy repented that he had been the first warrior to stick his spear in the chest of one of the two white people in Akeri. The Masai name for Akeri, where the two missionaries were murdered, is "Keringo". Ole Darpoy admitted that they had nothing against the missionaries, apart from the fact that it was his duty as a warrior to defend the land. According to Rev. Maliaki M. Lukumay, Ole Darpoy was touched in his heart by the words in the hymn *"Era Engai an Enyorata"* (God is Love), sung almost every day by Masai children in the baptism class. The words of this song, sung in Maa, made him seek out the teacher who was teaching the catechumens at Ketumbeine in Central Masai. Told that God loved the world and gave his only Son, so that whoever believes in him shall not perish, he agreed to join the baptism class in his old age.

On the day of his baptism, he told the young and old Masai people who were present to follow Jesus because there was no other way except to believe in the risen Lord. On August 5, 1962, Ole Darpoy threw away his old name at the age of 96 and took the Christian name Paulos Mukaine.[19] At this baptism, the presence of missionary Carl W. Johnson, a "mzungu", caused Ole Paulos Mukaine to remember once again the killing of the missionaries Ovir and Segebrock in (Keringo) Akeri.[20]

---

18 Ibidem
19 Rev. Maleaki M Lukumay, report, in: Umoja Northern Diocese Magazine, Oct. 1962, No. 23
20 Ibidem

The Germans built a Boma (fortification) in 1900, using the sweat and blood of Ilarusa men and women as another part of punishment. Askaris and German soldiers were stationed there, leaving the warriors in a state of despair. Missionary Leonard Blumer of Ilboru Mission Station reported that the proud Ilarusa warriors were forced to dig lime stone in the *boma la chokaa* (limestone fort) with their spears. Their beautifully decorated shields were used as wheelbarrows to carry stone and mud to the building site in Arusha. With their swords, they cut huge trees for the purpose of burning limestone. Women were forced to bring banana fibers for thatching, while older women pounded mud with their feet for building purposes. Others were to bring good grass daily for the donkeys of "the great lord" (*Bwana mkubwa*) at the Boma.[21] "Since that time the Ilarusa warriors have learned to bow their heads to their masters", wrote Blumer. Every warrior had to work at least seven to eight hours daily. Hatred and enmity was buried deep in their hearts, but superficially they were a changed people.

Missionaries Müller, Fabmann, Krause, and Fickert visit Olkaris Sabaya Ilaiser of Boru

In spite of the tragic incident in Akeri on the night of October 19-20, 1896, the Leipzig missionaries resumed activity in Meru land. Meru land gained a special feeling in the hearts of many missionaries. In 1901, the Leipzig Missionary Society felt that the awaited time to evangelize the Wameru had come. The German Boma in Arusha offered safety and assurance for a new start. Avoiding their plot in Akeri, missionaries Krause and Fickert founded a new station at a place called Nkoaranga, near the homestead of Mangi Menauru, in March 1902. Krause had wanted to build a station in Akeri, but Mangi Menauru was hesitant to allow the missionaries to build their station far away from his homestead for two reasons: first of all, Akeri was already deserted, and secondly, Menauru was himself not sure that he could guarantee their safety (ELMB, 1902: 276). In July 1902, nissionaries Müller and Faßmann, accompanied by the missionaries of Nkoaranga station and porters from Machame, reconnoitered the possibility of extending work to the Ilarusa. They wanted to see the land and meet with the chiefs (ibid: 391).

Their prime aim was to visit Mangi Sabaya at his homestead at Marikanda in Boru, near

---

21   Tagebuch de Missionstation Ilboru von Missionar Leonard Blumer, 4. Oktober 1922: *„Mit ihren Speeren muß-ten sie die Kalksteine brechen und auf ihren Schilden dann hierhertragen, wo der Kalk dann gebrannt wurde. Das Brennholz mußten sie ringsum //in der Steppe// zusammensuchen und mit ihren großen Seitenmessern fällen. Von hier wurde dann der gebrannte Kalk nach Arusha für die Festungsbauten (= boma) hingetragen. Seit der Zeit sind die Arushaleute erst endgültig gezähmt."* Compare Dr. Carl Uhling, Mitteilungen aus den Deutschen Schutzgebieten, Berlin, 1909: 249: *„Die bedeutendste der Merulandschaften ist Aruscha, namentlich seitdem dort im Jahre 1900 ein Militärposten angelegt worden ist. Der Militärposten Arusha hat das Aussehen der Land-schaft wesentlich verändert. Die geräumige 'Boma', das Fort, ist im Rechteck angelegt, von einer Opuntien und Stacheldrahthecke, einem mannestiefen Graben und einer starken Mauer mit Bastionen umgeben. Im Innern dieser Befestigung liegen in sehr praktischer Anordnung die Magazine und die Wohnräume der Besatzung, die aus einem Leutnant, einem Sanitätsunteroffizier und etwa 30 Askaris, schwarzen Soldaten, besteht. Der Posten hat ei-genes Vieh und einen eigenen Gemüsegarten. Der Bedarf des Postens hat in der Nähe der Boma ein Dorf entstehen lassen, dessen Häuser an geraden Straßen im Küstenstil erbaut sind. Außer Eingeborenen wohnen Küstenneger und Inder im Dorfe als Händler."*

the present Ilboru congregation. Before this, they reported their presence on the land to the officials of the Boma in Arusha. Missionary Krause of Nkoaranga mentioned that Lieutenant Küster, officer in charge of the Boma, gave them a warm welcome. A small village was beginning to grow around the Boma with small shops that sold commodities that were also available in Moshi (ibidem). Asked about the current situation in Arusha, Lt. Küster gave no answer to missionary Müller. Whether the Ilarusa were on friendly terms with the Wazungu or not, Lt. Küster did not know. Küster had been transferred to Arusha only two weeks before this visit.

Küster escorted the missionaries to the homestead of Mangi Sabaya Ilaiser, where they spent a night. Mangi Sabaya received them in an unexpectedly friendly manner, giving them food and whatever help they needed. In spite of Mangi Sabaya's friendly and charming mood, Müller placed little confidence in him. He reported that no one among the four Europeans could sleep a wink for fear of a surprise attack by the Ilarusa warriors. Throughout the night, they took turns keeping guard. The next day they surveyed the neighbouring land as far south as the land of Mangi Saruni. This exploratory journey convinced them that Arusha was a fertile land with many streams. To their surprise, they saw irrigation furrows dug by the natives. Their return journey led them through the "*Kambi ya chokaa*", where the Ilarusa warriors had been forced to extract limestone when the Arusha Boma was built. Krause mentioned the census that had been carried out by the German colonial government in 1902. The population of Meru was about 5,506, while Arusha had a population of about 8,365 (ibidem). In both cases, Krause remarked, the population would have been higher had it not been for the wars. He mentioned that many *shambas* were uninhabited. Following this visit to Arushaland, Krause was assigned the task of locating an appropriate plot in Arusha. The demarcation of this plot was completed in January 1904 (ibid: 391).

References

Bainton, Roland H. (1950) The Church of Our Fathers, New York, Westminister Press

Gulliver, Paul (1963) Social control in an African society: Study of the Arusha, agricultural Masai of northern Tanganyika, London, Routledge

Iliffe, John (1969) Tanganyika under German Rule 1905-1912, Cambridge: University Press

Merker, Moritz (1910) Die Masai, Berlin, Reimer

Müller, Emil (1896) Tagebuch der Missionsstation Madschame vom 11-13 Oct. 1896

Müller, Emil (1936) "Aus der Tiefe in die Höh, Segebrock und Ovir, unsere Blutzeugen am Meru", Leipzig, Verlag der Ev.-Luth. Mission

Nelson, Anton (1967) The Freemen of Meru, London, New York, 9-11

Parsalaw, J.W. (1999) A History of the Church, Diocese in the Arusha Region from 1904 to 1958. Erlangen, Erlanger Verlag für Mission und Ökumene

Saibull, Solomon Ole; Carr, Rachel (1981) Herd and Spear. The Maasai of East Africa, London, Collins and Harvill Press

Evangelisch-Lutherisches Missionsblatt, Leipzig, 1897

Evangelisch-Lutherisches Missionsblatt, Leipzig, 1902

Evangelisch-Lutherisches Missionsblatt, Leipzig, 1925

Evangelisch-Lutherisches Missionsblatt, Leipzig, 1940

Moni Parisius

125 years of contested memory. A Discourse Analysis of the Reception of the Killing of two Leipzig Missionaries from a Postcolonial Perspective

Introduction

During my long-term internship with Leipzig Mission (LMW), my attention was drawn to the tragic events that happened at Mt. Meru when I saw the artwork dedicated to Ovir and Segebrock in the mission house chapel. The hand-carved wooden Makonde cross was given to the Leipzig Mission in 1993 by Paulo Akyoo, at that time Bishop of the Meru Diocese, as a symbol of reconciliation and forgiveness.

While I was working in the LMW archives, studying antique mission reports, I realized how differently things were talked about in the late 19th century. I then began to wonder how the story could be told today from a postcolonial perspective. My goal was to prove the bias that the "martyr legend" was based on and, in doing so, deconstruct the false and prejudiced notion of White, European victims. I want to draw a different picture, one that underlines European aggression and native defense.

1. Theoretical framework

The methodological basis of my research was discourse analysis. To analyze a discourse, one needs to clearly define what a discourse is and what fragments it is formed of. My analysis sought to examine statements within the discourse, the main arguments, and which stylistic means were used to underpin those.

The central question of this discourse analysis is the connection between political, social and institutional structures and power dynamics and their linguistic expression in the form of texts. The discursive approach is used to examine how the knowledge produced by a particular discourse is linked to power and how practices are regulated, identities are constructed, as well as ways of representing identities, how certain events, objects and subjects are represented and how they are thought about and studied (Kossek, 2003).

Before diving deeper into the topic, I want to make some introductory notes, as I think it is important to critically reflect my own position. As a White, able-bodied European, I can only speak from my own perspective. I can never be truly neutral. During the time I have spent researching for this paper, I have also reflected upon my personal entanglement as a descendant of a Lutheran missionary who was working in Southern Africa. I came to realize that even though young people like me are part of a new generation and may be less bound to conventional patterns of thinking and traditional organizational structures, we should not think of ourselves as any less bound to racist and colonial structures that shape our thoughts and actions because we grew up in an equally racist and colonialist society.

2. Literature analysis

For a historic analysis that tries to unearth what happened, primary sources, like the letters of the two missionaries Müller and Faßmann, would have the greatest value since they are internal documents, written mainly for the purpose of informing their superiors as accurately as possible. For a discourse analysis however, publications - made for swaying public opinion – are the most valuable. In the following chapter, I want to briefly give insights on a few publications that were formative for the discourse. For clearer structuring, I have decided to divide the discourse into five phases.

2.1. Damage Control

Directly after the incident, the mission publications described it more like a tragic accident or natural disaster, without demonizing the African locals and with only moderate adoration for the two missionaries. Just three weeks after the killings, a sermon was delivered by mission director Karl von Schwartz that can be seen as the beginning of the martyr legend. In this sermon, the situation of the mission was compared to that of a victorious commander who, through the deaths of his soldiers, was incited to continue the fight instead of giving up. (Altena, 2003) This is in essence the goal of this kind of representation of Segebrock and Ovir, to redefine the mournful event into a positive outcome.

The predominant publications of that era were von Schwartz' "Segebrock und Ovir. Zwei früh vollendete Missionare" (1897) and the mission reports of the years 1896 and 1897. One main focus of these texts is the attempt to deflect criticism of the entanglement with the German colonial forces. They try to achieve that with two main strategies: either by blaming the supposed inherent depravity of the locals or by portraying the killings as an unfathomable act of God. The idea that the too-close contact with Captain Johannes was the reason is pointedly avoided. "May the joyful sacrifice of their young lives spur us all on to erect a lasting memorial to them through sacrificial and joyful support of the mission for which they died" (von Schwartz, 1897: 19). This quotation shows how quickly the Leipzig Mission ideologically and economically capitalized on the deaths of their missionaries. "Now more than ever" is what sums up the defiant attitude towards missionary activities in the contested region of Mt. Meru. The possible author of the "martyr legend" was Mission director Karl von Schwartz. The pragmatic motivation is clear. Von Schwartz had to turn the narrative around to save the fledgling African mission, the financial support of the LMW's other projects, and his own career.

2.2. Shifting the Focus

The second phase can be roughly narrowed down to the epoch from 1902 until 1920. This time can be summarized as "shifting the focus". It was the time when German colonial reign had been firmly established. Publications from that period, such as Adolphi's "Am Fuße der Bergriesen Ostafrikas" and Weishaupt's "Ostafrikanische Wandertage", try to downplay the events as initial difficulties and put much more emphasis on the, in their view, positive outcome, the establishment of a mission station, and the supposed pacification in the Meru region. For instance, Adolphi, regarding Captain Johannes' punitive expedition, affirms that the secular authorities must act in this way in order to not endanger the reputation of the government. Reputation in this case can only mean fear of brutal punishment, on which the rule is based. Martin Weishaupt firmly holds on to the central theme that Akeri is a "consecrated site for the Leipzig Mission" (Weishaupt, 1913: 53), he also states that the true reasons for the murder cannot be established with absolute certainty and even acknowledges that the initially widely accepted explanation that the attackers acted out of mere greed is wrong. Instead, he quotes inhabitants of the Meru region who say that the Ilarusa wanted to prevent the settlement of Europeans (ibid). It is interesting to see what conclusions he draws from that. Instead of questioning the European presence in East Africa, he claims that the indigenous warriors were not fighting against humans but against God and that "God returns wherever He is expelled." (ibid)

2.3. Veneration and Glorification

The loss of German colonial territories in 1920 marks a turning point in the presentation of the Akeri killings. In 1922, the grave and monument in Akeri were renewed to keep the memory alive. As German nationalism grew in the following decade, the heroic and saint-like depictions of Segebrock and Ovir also reached their peak. It seems as if the writers and readers of texts from that time were longing for Heroic epics and stories of infallible martyrs rather than taking a critical look at the past. The 1936 text "Blutzeugen am Meru" is typical of that. The text gives the impression of a subsumption of the individuals under the narrative. The focus is often more on the negative depiction of non-Europeans, the supposed benefits of colonialism, and the "loss" of the German colonies. Perhaps inevitably, the text that most glorifies Ovir and Segebrock also treats them predominantly as symbols.

In 1946, for the 50th anniversary of the Akeri killings, Pastor Ranft dedicated a poem to the memory of the events at Mt. Meru. The poem is a literal hymn of praise to Missionary Ovir, which lacks any claim to a differentiated or historically accurate portrayal and instead strives to stylize the deceased as a martyr and "venerate" him – rather untypical for Lutherans – as a saint. It was not printed and published, but I assume it was recited in a liturgical context. The target group is therefore quite different from that of books, rather poorly educated but probably pietistic. In 1946, these people wanted to be distracted from the present post-war horrors and therefore enjoyed the heroic epic of times long past. I think that the influence of informal texts such as Ranft's poem on the general discourse is not insignificant compared to that of official publications, for example, those in the mission reports. In the public's mind, a presentation in the form of artful lyrics is probably more likely to take root than complex explanations in a report or piece of literature.

2.4. Entering the postcolonial era

What followed the above-described "veneration phase" can be most accurately characterized as an "epoch of silence". Whether consciously, due to an honest feeling of remorse, or unconsciously, simply because after the Second World War and later in the GDR other things were prioritized, is not fully clear from today's perspective. Literature about the Akeri incident was not published, and Segebrock and Ovir were not talked about too much. Thus, the discourse did not experience notable alterations. What had been firmly established in the minds of most people, the Martyr Legend, survived for decades and is, to some extent, still found today. The current situation can be described as "entering the postcolonial era". While some writers and readers are still in the phase of silence, others try to actively deconstruct old colonial narratives and push the discourse in a more historically grounded and power-critical direction. Prof. Joseph Parsalaw was the first scholar to pay sufficient attention to the socio-political conditions prevalent in the Meru region. His chapter on the Akeri killings paved the way for the discourse to change (Parsalaw, 1999).

Thorsten Altena describes the deliberate stylization of Segebrock and Ovir as martyrs and suggests the reasons for this, namely, the fear of losing financial support and the hope of recruiting new missionary candidates through the heroic portrayal (Altena, 2003: 282-285).

Conclusion

An outcome that I was very sure to encounter in my analysis is a perceptible paradigm shift in the interpretation patterns that were used to talk and write about the Akeri killings. I expected to find that change in academic literature as well as in common mission publications. I was rather surprised that I did not find a notable change, in the sense of an alteration of the discourse, that would question the depiction of Ovir and Segebrock as heroes and martyrs. The discourse remained fairly static and did not evolve into a self-critical direction that would have allowed other narratives for a long time. My explanation for this phenomenon is that the power structures that dictate how knowledge is transmitted are widely unchanged. Still today, large parts of our cognition come from a European viewpoint. I would describe the current situation as a backlog of discourse.

When looking at protestant mission over the past centuries since its emergence in the 18th century, one constant can be observed: its constant self-justification. No Christian religious activity has been so compelled to explain its own existence as the Christianization in other parts of the world, then as now. And not without reason; after all, then as now, only a timid renunciation of colonial crimes had taken place, if at all, pure lip service. So, when will Christian mission begin to genuinely detach itself from problematic entanglements instead of seeking justifications for them?

I ask myself whether – from a postcolonial perspective – reconciliation is a goal we should long for. The striving for reparation must be an honest one and must never be motivated by the desire to "cleanse" oneself of shameful deeds. Who is even in a position to demand forgiveness and reconciliation?

Colonized people and places could only be objects of colonization processes because knowledge about them has been assessed in a certain way. Colonial discourses have formed the perception of the colonized as "colonizable". Obtaining information and spreading it is an instrument of colonial rule. Colonial rule itself is expressed by the power to define oneself and others (German: "Definitionsmacht"). Decolonization processes are made possible when we begin to reverse this strategy. Recognizing that all people have this power to (re)define can be a momentum of self-empowerment for the formerly colonized.

It is important to note that postcolonial discourse is not about countering the "wrong" construction of the colonized, the female, the black, etc. with the "right" one but about helping the subaltern to become a subject by making their perspective audible (Castro-Varela/ Dhawan, 2020).

I think it is helpful to demystify European knowledge for what it actually is: just one of many contextual systems of knowledge. And thus, by no means universal but rather provincial.

In order to meet the challenge of a postcolonial, globalized world, the current relations of discrimination and domination need confrontational-dialogical debates in order to name and change injustices, especially in practices of education and pedagogy (Salgado, 2019). Power-critical education and global learning are keys to a new information culture that does not reproduce colonial discourses. The aim of postcolonial education should be to enable people to engage in a retrospective reformulation and reconfiguration of capitalist modernity and its integral links with colonization processes in a global context.

Colonialism divided the world into centers and peripheries. Today, all over the planet, societies are yearning for a shift in the centers of power to redress an imbalance that has grown over centuries. As Kenyan writer Ngugi wa Thiong'o notes, this must happen on two levels. On the one hand, between nations, that is, shifting the center from its taken-for-granted position in the West to a multitude of spheres in all cultures of the world; on the other hand, also within each nation. In almost all nations, power lies with the ruling class of society, a cis-male, bourgeois minority (Thiong'o, 2017).

I believe that the discourse is still "alive", and it is open for alterations by anyone who contributes insights on the Akeri killings. The postcolonial phase has just begun. Though arguably colonialism is not over, it has only changed its shape. But for the first time, the majority of people in Western countries would fully agree that colonialism is immoral and that their societies shouldn't benefit from and produce global inequalities. This situation invites us to critically re-evaluate history and gain new knowledge. Though this knowledge is not the final goal, it is also meant to support the anti-colonial struggles of today.

References

Adolphi, Heinrich (1903) Am Fuße der Bergriesen Ostafrikas, Leipzig, Verlag der Ev.-Luth. Mission.

Altena, Thorsten (2003) "Ein Häuflein Christen mitten in der Heidenwelt des dunklen Erdteils". Zum Selbst- und Fremdverständnis protestantischer Missionare im kolonialen Afrika 1884-1918. Münster, Wachsmann.

Castro Varela, María do Mar; Dhawan, Nikita (2020) Postkoloniale Theorie. Eine kritische Einführung, Bielefeld, Transcript.

Fanon, Frantz (1983) Schwarze Haut, Weiße Masken, Frankfurt, Surkamp.

Kossek, Brigitte (2003) "Post/koloniale Diskurse". In: Afrikanische Diaspora – out of Afrika into the World, ed. Werner Zips, Münster, LIT-Verlag.

Parsalaw, Joseph (1999) A history of the Lutheran Church, Diocese in the Arusha Region from 1904 to 1958, Erlangen, Verlag für Mission und Ökumene.

Salgado, Rubia (ed.) (2019) Pädagogik im Globalen postkolonialen Raum, Weinheim Basel, Beltz.

Schwartz, Karl von; Handmann, Richard (ed.) (1896) Evangelisch-Lutherisches Missionsblatt. Jahrgang 1896, Leipzig, Verlag der Ev.-Luth. Mission.

Schwartz, Karl von (1897) Karl Segebrock und Ewald Ovir. Zwei früh vollendete Missionare, Leipzig, Verlag der Evangelisch-Lutherischen Mission.

Schwartz, Karl von; Handmann, Richard (ed.) (1897) Evangelisch-Lutherisches Missionsblatt. Jahrgang 1897, Leipzig, Verlag der Ev.-Luth. Mission.

Thiong'o, Ngũgĩ wa (2017) Moving the Centre, Münster, Unrast.

Weishaupt, Martin (1913) Ostafrikanische Wandertage, Leipzig, Verlag der Evangelisch-Lutherischen Mission.

Kristina Ecis

Rediscovery and reevaluation of mission understanding of the Courland Lutheran Consistory and missionary martyr Karl Segebrock

In 1942, Latvian Lutheran Foreign Mission Secretary Roberts Feldmanis (1942) wrote that while mission work from Latvia was suspended due to war, the Church should lay a foundation for the next mission thrust when it would be possible again. However, for the next 55 years, due to Soviet occupation, foreign mission from Latvia was impossible and the Church in Latvia forgot its mission history. In the magazine of the Leipzig Mission dedicated to the tragic events at Mt. Meru 125 years ago, its director Ravinder Salooja (2021) asked a question about the two unknown names of the locals who were killed – didn't they count? The same question can be asked about Karl Segebrock, as he was also forgotten in his land of birth. Therefore, today it is a task to rediscover our mission roots and remember the martyr Karl Segebrock from Jelgava (Mitau).

Two hundred years ago, the Baltic territory was legally a part of the Russian Empire. In 1832, a new law was introduced regarding Evangelical Lutheran Churches in Russia, which created the Consistory of Courland, alongside seven others (Rozentāls, 2012). Due to some colonial history from the 13th century, the Baltics historically had close connections with Germany. During the 19th and early 20th century, the majority of Lutherans in Courland were ethnic Latvians (Germans were only 1/18, or 5.5% of all Lutherans) (Mühlenbachs, 1922), but most of the pastors were Baltic Germans, which caused complex power and relational struggles on the national level. By the middle of the 19th century, some young Latvian men were able to obtain a university education, and a portion of them became pastors in the Courland Lutheran Consistory.

The research question for this paper is the reevaluation of the Courland Consistory's mission understanding, its connections with the Leipzig Mission, and how these factors inspired pastors in Courland. The emphasis is also on Karl Segebrock, as he is virtually unknown in the Latvian Lutheran Church today. The paper also studies both the similarities and differences present in the way the Baltic German and Latvian publications covered the Mount Meru event.

The method of research is content analysis, searching for keywords "mission", "gentile mission" (Heidenmission), and "Segebrock", as well as the hermeneutical method of interpreting the protocols of synods and newspaper publications in the historical, cultural, and theological context of the time.

The reevaluation of mission understanding of the Courland Consistory

After the Livonian state was dissolved, the last master of the Livonian Order, Gotthard Kettler, became the first duke of Courland and Semigallia (Courland for short) in 1561. The duchy existed as a vassal state of Poland until 1795, when it was incorporated into the Russian Empire as a Governorate of Courland. Courland was predominantly Lutheran due to close ties with the reformers in Germany (Feldmanis, 2011).

The consistory of Courland had regular synods. The main sources for reevaluation of the mission understanding of the Lutheran Church of Courland are the synod minutes published by the consistories themselves, which can partially be found in the archive of the Evangelical Lutheran Church of Latvia (ELCL), as well as the archive of the Latvian National Library.

The best information on the beginnings of foreign mission in Courland Consistory can be found in the 1885 synod minutes, which was called the Jubilee or 50th synod, therefore, allowing the conclusion that the Courland Consistory was formed in 1835. The matter of foreign mission was discussed by two authors: pastors Ludwig Katterfeld and Reinhard Räder.

Katterfeld (1885) provided an overview of domestic mission and diaconia work, only passingly mentioning the significance of foreign or heathen mission. In the 15th synod (1850), Pastor Hillner introduced a matter on how to promote the work of domestic missions and the establishment of deaconia on the basis of the evangelical tradition of the priesthood of all believers. Further, Katterfeld stated that Hillner, Talsi Pastor Tiling, and the pastors of the Piltene district submitted a proposal to make the domestic mission a constant topic of each synod, as well as suggesting that similar interest should also be shown for foreign missions.

However, the pastor from Kuldīga, Räder, provided a more complete overview of the beginnings of foreign mission in Courland Consistory. In this jubilee synod, he, as the Speaker General of the heathen (Heiden) mission, reported on missions in Courland, pointing out that it had already been done for 48 years (much earlier than mentioned by Katterfeld). In his report, he pointed out the foreign missions in Courland, comparing them with a river that receives water from various sources. He divided the overview of foreign mission in three periods, each consisting of sixteen years (Lamberg, 1885).

The first ideas of foreign mission in 1837–1852 came from the pastor of Jelgava St. Trinity Church, Friedrich Eduard Neander (1802–1895), who invited the church members to participate in ministry with their gifts of love. In 1837, Pastor Neander had started a special accounting registry for mission donations, and until 1852, the annual donations of church members made up an average of 300 roubles. The second source of missionary thought mentioned came from Talsi Pastor Tilling, who personally knew the missionary Krone and not only collected donations himself, but also invited other pastors to do the same (Lamberg, 1885).

In synods held in Courland, matters on foreign missions were initially brought forth by Pastor Neander in 1842 and 1845, and later by Balgale Pastor Krause and the above-mentioned Tilling, who in 1852, submitted to the synod 12 theses so that foreign missions would be a permanent topic of synod (Lamberg, 1885). Since Neander and Tilling knew missionaries, for the initial six years the donations were sent to Barmer Mission (as Ryland, 2013 states, Barmer or Rheinish Misison sent missionaries to Southwest Africa to serve with the Herero, Namah, Damra and Khoisan tribes). Later, donations were mostly sent to the Dresden and Leipzig Mission (Lamberg, 1885).

Räder further pointed out the second period of foreign mission in Courland Consistory (1853–1869), which he considered to be the period of the organization of mission activity. During this time, in the synod of 1856, Pastor Neander became the chief speaker of the heathen mission. Participating in this synod was also the director of the Leipzig Mission at the time, Dr. Karl Friedrich Leberecht Graul. Looking at the protocol of that year, it is possible to conclude that Dr. Graul gave an uplifting message about foreign mission, which facilitated Pastor Krause to remind others of the 1852 synod decision to have foreign mission as a permanent topic of discussion at the synods. Donations were given by several churches in Courland; Pastor Grüner of Bārbele was tasked with the publication of a mission appendix in Latvian to supplement the newspaper Latviešu Avīzes (Wilpert, 1856); and in 1866, a mission festival was celebrated in the Sēlpils district. The average annual donations at the time reached 1,200 roubles, most of which were sent to support the work of the Leipzig Mission. Soon after the death of missionary Krone, the synod made a decision in 1865 that all donations to foreign mission should be sent to Leipzig from then on (Weide 1882). To promote a more thorough cooperation between the Courland Consistory and the Leipzig Mission, Director Julius Hardeland of the Leipzig Mission participated in the 1863 synod in Jelgava (Mitau). Räder also noted that since the former foreign mission speaker Neander believed that a sector of foreign mission had been established, he could step down from the office, and Räder was voted in (Lamberg, 1885).

In Räder's opinion, the third stage of foreign mission (1869–1855) resembled a slowly flowing river with developing missions: Hardeland arrived in Courland twice more (in 1874 and 1882); mission festivals took place; churches participated in donating towards mission; and the annual volume of donations increased to 1,900 roubles. Of all 199 churches in the consistory, only 8 churches had not given any donations to mission — 5 of which were located in Lithuania and 3 in Courland. Räder saw mission festivals as the main strategy for the promotion of foreign missions among church members.

It can be concluded from the minutes of the synod that the chief speakers of synods for foreign mission in the course of the years were Neander (1845, 1857–1862), Krause (1848), Tilling (1852, 1855), Räder (1870–1882, and 1885), and Lösewitz (1862), as well as mission directors Dr. Graul (1856–1857) and Hardeland (1863, 1865–1869, 1882–1884) (Lamberg, 1885).

In 1894, Heinrich Johann Seesemann, the pastor in Zaļenieki (Grünhof), became the mission speaker, but he provided reports on activity in foreign mission already in 1893 (Boettcher, 1893, 1894). The 1897 protocol mentions the deaths of Karl Segebrock and Evald Ovir, but nothing more is described there. Most likely, the reason for this omission is that by the time the synod happened, the event had already been talked about among the pastors. The report of Pastor Seeseman finished with a note of hope as a young man from Courland, Fritz Stamberg (Fricis Štambergs 1871-1957), had started mission studies in Leipzig (Boettcher, 1897). Pastor Seesemann continued to speak on mission in the subsequent synods. It is important to notice that he not only gave statistics on the finances sent to Leipzig, but also tried to give more theological background for mission. In the 1898 report, he mentions the work of the founder of modern missiology, German Dr. Gustav Warneck "Evangelische Missionslehre", which demonstrates that pastors of the Courland consistory were regularly educated in the area of mission work (Panck, 1898). In 1901, the mission secretary gave a report on mission history, mentioning that the French Revolution, Methodists in England, and Pietists in Germany prepared the ground for great mission work in the 19th century. He mentioned the new colonial politics of the European powers fostering mission work as a positive way of supporting mission work (Panck, 1901).

Pastor Ernests Freibergs (1954) later pointed out that since approximately 1896, several pastors created the "Courland Foreign Mission Conference" in which they met from time to time, read reports on foreign mission and organized foreign mission festivals. Courland Consistory continued working and sending donations to Leipzig Mission until ELCL officially stopped cooperation with Leipzig Mission after World War I (Lauciņš, 2015). The only exception was Kuldīga Church, which continued sending donations to Leipzig with a special consent from the ELCL synod in order to support a missionary from there, the above-mentioned Štambergs who ministered in Tanzania (Freibergs, 1954).

From the examined minutes, it is clear that an awareness of the necessity for foreign mission was regularly cultivated among Lutheran pastors of Courland. However, the minutes, at least the early ones, do not really provide the theological basis for mission, rather showing that foreign mission is important, should be financially supported, and that missionaries should be prayed for. Following the spirit of the time, Courland Synod used the term 'heathen' (Heiden) mission and did not see any problem with colonial powers dividing Africa and other new lands and supporting mission. Räder also pointed out the activity of the Holy Spirit, which glorifies His Name, and stated that God is a faithful and merciful Shepherd who gathers His restless herd, all of which can be seen as a part of the Missio Dei concept that was developed later in the 20th century (Lamberg, 1885).

It can also be concluded that the Lutheran Consistory of Courland had strong ties with the Leipzig Mission Society. The ties were strengthened by the visits of mission directors and sharing at the synods. These close ties then provided missionary carrier opportunities for candidates from Courland, including Karl Segebrock, who will be introduced next.

Karl Segebrock – missionary martyr from Courland

On October 30, 1896, among diverse topics on the 3rd page in the newspaper Latviešu Avīzes ("Latvian Newspaper"), there was the following news item by an author m.:

> *Missionaries killed. Quite sad news reached us last week from faraway East Africa. Not far from Meru mission station in the Kilimanjaro area on October 20th (Nov. 1st), two young, zealous preachers of Christ's Gospel, both sons of the Baltics, Karl Segebrock from Jelgava and Ewald Ovir from Revel, of whose blessed work with the gentiles we just provided an article to our dear readers (see No. 39 of Baznīca un Skola), were killed by the natives (savages). Only less than a year ago, the Leipzig Mission Society sent them there to fight for Christ's Kingdom, and they took the job with great zeal. Therefore, the sad news has painfully shocked everyone who cares for our evangelical mission. May God comfort the relatives of the murdered young men! A military unit has been sent from the colony German East Africa to reprimand the doers of this terrible work (author's translation).*

This year marks 125 years since this sad event. As mentioned above, due to many historical reasons, the names of these zealous young men have been forgotten. Therefore, it is time to ask, who was Karl Segebrock? One of the reasons he was completely forgotten is that there are almost no materials about him in his land of birth. There are some publications in Latvian and German newspapers that will be examined in the last part, but those provide very scarce personal information about him. The largest amount of information on Karl Segebrock, his life, and his ministry can be found in the archive of the Leipzig Mission Society, which is available at the Francke Foundation in Halle.

When examining the protocols of the synods over a longer period of time, it was possible to notice that foreign mission was promoted when there was at least one pastor who was "on fire" for it. This pastor then reported about foreign mission during the synods and invited others to take part in it. We can see that influence also in the life of Karl Segebrock.

Karl Segebrock was born in the capital city of Courland, Jelgava (Mitau), on January 4, 1872. His father was a carpenter, and he had an older brother (here and further on, Segebrock's biography data was taken from his personal application to the Leipzig Missionary Society, Segebrock 1889; Schwartz, 1897). He studied at the elementary school and then later at the regional school. Already during his school years, he found out about mission work. During that time, the pastor in Jelgava (Mitau) St. John church was Ludwig Katterfeld (1843–1910), whose report about mission work in the Courland Synod of 1885 shows his deep passion for foreign mission (Katterfeld, 1885). Segebrock wrote that in his St. John church, he heard a passionate sermon of a missionary and therefore decided to become a missionary himself. All of this points to Segebrock attending a church where mission's passion was nurtured and promoted.

After finishing his schooling, Segebrock took confirmation classes, where his knowledge about Bible history and catechism was evaluated as "very good". After that, he was confirmed on Palm Sunday in 1887. After the confirmation, Karl mentioned to his pastor that he wanted to become a missionary to bring the light of the gospel to those who hadn't heard yet. This wish itself was not enough; in order to test Karl's perseverance and talent, he had to work as a teacher's assistant for one year at a church school. In his work, the young man showed passion and diligence, and his trial year was done excellently. Therefore, on Easter in 1889, Karl Segebrock was admitted to the mission school in Leipzig at the age of 17.

The Leipzig Mission Society was established in 1836. Its mission fields at the end of the 19th century were in India, where they worked among the Tamil people, as well as in British and German East African colonies (today's Tanzania). At the time Karl went to Leipzig, the work in Africa had just started (Baznīcas Vēstnesis, 1897).

Segebrock spent six years in the mission seminar. Von Schwartz (1897) mentions that because Segebrock was coming from the Baltics, where there was a different culture, some things in the seminar seemed formal, even pedantic, and small. Because he himself was a teacher before, it was initially difficult initially to be a student again, who must obey the rules. He understood, however, that he was in missionary training and that he needed to prepare for much more complicated situations in the mission field. Later, he was thankful for the years spent in the missions school, even including the difficulties.

It is very interesting to notice that while in the seminar in Leipzig, sometimes Segebrock and Ovir were called "Russians" ("Russen") (Schwartz, 1897), even though they were ethnically Baltic Germans who came from places where the major populations were Latvians and Estonians, not Russians. The question of nationality and struggles in the language and national level will be discussed in the last part of the paper.

Overall, it seems that Segebrock was a good student, passing his final examinations in February and March 1895, before being ordained as a missionary at the Ordination Service on June 2, 1895. Soon after that, he received his commission to the mission field with the Wachagga people in East Africa (Evangelisch-Lutherische Mission zu Leipzig, 1895). He started his journey to his mission field on June 17, 1895, at the age of 23, together with a missionary from today's Estonia, Ewald Ovir. As mentioned before, until this point, Segebrock's biography was basically unknown, as most of these references were available in Germany. From now on, the facts from this portion of Segebrock's life can also be found in publications in the territory of Latvia.

In August, they arrived in British-controlled Mombasa, and on September 2nd, they started their two and a half-week, 300 km-long journey inwards on the continent to Mamba in the Kilimanjaro area. Segebrock makes notes in his diary about this journey, which was full of difficulties and the dangers of war. Missionaries were warned not to go inland without military guards (Segebrock, 1897a). They had to learn patience, as the journey was very slow, sometimes even experiencing misunderstandings from the guides and porters. They were taken by the heat of Africa and the strike of the local paid helpers. On the way, Segebrock also got sick with a high fever (Segebrock, 1897b). They finally arrived on September 19th (Segebrock, 1897c). Segebrock started his ministry at the Mamba mission station, and missionary Althaus was his senior supervisor and helper in the first stages of ministry (Segebrock, 1895a). While at his mission station, Segebrock was learning the local languages, leading services, and starting to preach the gospel. With great joy, he wrote at the end of the year to Leipzig that he was able to do the Christmas sermon in the local language, even though he still recognized that he needed more language training (Segebrock, 1895b).

After around one year of ministry, Segebrock and Ovir received an invitation to expand mission work to the territory of Meru land, with the Arusha and Maasai tribes – approximately 80 km west. In October 1896, they started their way to Mt. Meru. On the one hand, both missionaries had done good work at their mission stations, as they had met people and started to share the Gospel („Tēvijas Kalendāra" redakcija, 1899). On the other hand, Ovir wrote in a letter that they understood that near Mt. Meru, there would be great challenges. They considered it a great honor to be chosen to establish a new mission station after being in service for only one year, realizing that in the new place there would not be any European commodities and that their mission would be a pioneering frontier mission. They both confessed great trust in God's guidance, and their greatest motivation was that nobody else had preached the gospel there. Ovir wrote in his letter: "So the life in a tent continues for me and Segebrock until we build a house. Sometimes it could become quite lonely, because we are separated from the European settlements and civilization by a lonely steppe. I am glad that I have a country man and a friend together with me." (Ovir, 1896)

The missionaries were accompanied by 70 carriers from the local peoples. On October 15th, they arrived at Akeri at Mt. Meru and were treated very friendly by the leader of the Wameru tribe, Matunda. There was a German colonial unit led by Captain Johannes nearby. There was an attack during the night from October 19th to 20th, during which both missionaries, along with three Chagga civilians, were killed.

Latvian or Baltic German sources do not really have research or evaluation on the events and why they happened. There is more research done by other authors, for example, Dr. Joseph Wilson Parsalaw, Robert B. Munson, or the research of Dr. Moritz Fischer. With this martyrdom, the story of Karl Segebrock ends, but his legacy and zeal for mission should continue.

Mt. Meru event in Latvian and Baltic German publications – similarities and differences

This very sad event was noticed in both the Latvian and German press in the Baltics, but surprisingly, most of the time it was just a short death notice. This was the first such event, but initially only the German Goldingensher Anzeiger and the Latvian newspapers Tēvija and Latviešu Avīzes had short notices. A partial answer to this negligence, if such a word could be used, can be found in Pastor Katterfeld's letter to the Leipzig Mission Director, where he explains that the Russian government censor at first did not allow publishing the death notice, and only later changed his mind (Katterfeld, 1896). The other reason would be that, most likely at the time when the death notices were published, there was no sufficient information on what had actually happened.

Both Latvian newspapers gave very brief notices, for example:

> *Missionaries Karl Segebrock and Ewald Ovir, both Russian citizens, sent by the Leipzig Missionary Society, were killed by the natives on October 20th at Mount Meru, Kilimanjaro region. An expedition has been sent to punish the murderers. Segebrock was born in Jelgava, where his parents still live today. His father is the organist at the local Reformed church (author's translation). (Tēvija, 1896)*

Jelgava newspaper, quoted above, gave a little longer description using more explicit language – zealous preachers, native (savages), to fight for Christ's Kingdom.

A German newspaper refers to sources from The Telegraph about the fact of the murder: "Two sons of the Baltics, missionaries Karl Segebrock from Mitau and Ewald Ovir from Estonia, who were sent to East Africa by Leipzig Missionary Society, were murdered by the natives on November 1st (Oct. 20th) in Meru, Kilimanjaro area." (Goldingenscher Anzeiger, 1896). Then the Düna Zeitung and Revelischen Zeitung gave a slightly longer introduction to Segebrock and Ovir's lives, families and education. There was not, however, mention of retaliation mission or any military terms. The only other German publication in the early years was the report of Pastor Seesemann in 1897, mentioned in the first part of the paper.

After the initial messages were published, the next message in Latvian press was published in the Lutheran Church monthly magazine in December 1896. The description was not long and used similar strong language as had been in the Jelgava newspaper, with an added spiritual dimension, for example: "The evil enemy wants to scare and repel the churches of our motherland that just had sent its first messengers, but we will endure this test." There is also reference to the motive of martyrdom – "God will give, that through the death of these first martyrs, the churches of our motherland will be more moved towards the holy mission work." (Baznīcas Vēstnesis, 1896: 381) In the same magazine three months later, there is an overview about the Leipzig Mission, its beginnings and mission fields, the number of missionaries, and other statistics. The deaths of Ovir and Segebrock are briefly mentioned as a fact (Baznīcas Vēstnesis, 1897).

The longest explanation in Latvian was published in the Tēvzemes Kalendārs 1899. gadam. The editorial staff had finally received some personal letters, pictures, and diaries from Segebrock, yet there is almost no information about the early years of either Segebrock or Ovir. The longest explanation was about their work in Africa and the final night. Even though it is written in Latvian, the obvious source is a report from Captain Johannes, and the language used was strong:

> *The reason for the attack of the murderers, as can be understood till now, is possibly that the attackers did not want to tolerate Europeans living on their land, being afraid that they would be forced to work. Inhabitants there from Wadshagga, Waluash and Maasai tribes are not used to working, and they consider it slavery (author's translation). ("Tēvijas Kalendāra" redakcija, 1899: 10)*

At the end of the article, there is a challenge for Latvian young men to consider mission work. The authors mention that 9 Estonians have applied and want to serve, but there is only one Latvian man and one German lady from Riga serving ("Tēvijas Kalendāra" redakcija, 1899).

Echoes of this tragic event in Latvian publications can be found up until 1904, as Segebrock and Ovir are mentioned from time to time, when writing about mission work in Tanzania. Baznīcas Vēstnesis (1900) mentions the sad results of the German colonial punitive expedition and draws a conclusion that there is no greater hindrance to mission work than armed soldiers who say they protect it, instead causing people to be intimidated and upset, no longer trusting the words of peace. That is why the mission does not want the government's help from a position of power. The final report in this early period is a message of hope: seven years after the deaths of Segebrock and Ovir, in 1903, a Latvian from Kuldīga (Goldingen) Fricis Štambergs (Fritz Stamberg) is sent as a missionary to serve in the same area (Latviešu Avīzes, 1903).

The next time Segebrock and Ovir are mentioned is in 1936, on the 40th anniversary of their deaths. By that time, the independent Latvian Republic was established, and there was one Latvian Evangelical Lutheran Church, but it had separate Latvian churches with Bishop Kārlis Irbe and his successor Archbishop Teodors Grīnbergs and separate German churches with Bishop Peter Harald Poelchau (Latvijas evaņģēliskās luteriskās baznīcas draudžu mācītāju un priekšstāvju Sinodes sēžu Protokoli, 1922 and 1932). The Latvian Church newspaper Svētdienas Rīts (1936) published just a short note that 40 years had passed since their deaths and that their work was not in vain, as there was a growing Christian church there. Two German newspapers (Rigasche Post, 1936 and Rigasche Rundschau, 1936) give wider reports on the lives, ministries, and deaths of both men, as well as also mentioning the growing church there, in the same manner as the Latvian newspaper did. A memorial service was also held in Riga's St. Peter's Church. Evaluating the publications, it can be concluded that in reporting the event of the deaths, more information was given in the Latvian language. Most likely, it was assumed that German speakers could obtain information also outside of Courland. In the later years however, the German speakers were more concerned with the memory of Karl Segebrock than Latvians. Part of the reason could be that he was a Baltic German and not a Latvian. The other reason could be that the Latvian church in the 1920s stopped working together with the Leipzig Mission and started a partnership with the Swedish Church Mission, as was mentioned earlier.

However, in both the Latvian and German publications, there was no emphasis on the entanglement with the German colonial powers in East Africa, except for the one quote about sharing the Gospel using force. Officer Johannes is just mentioned as a part of events and the presence of the army unit is portrayed as more a coincidence than a regular situation. This could be connected with the political situation of Courland being part of the Russian Empire and the censorship of it, as both Latvians and Germans were minorities in a large Empire.

Conclusion

Karl Segebrock's life counted. As a young and passionate man at the age of 17, he went to Leipzig to study to become a missionary. At the age of 23, he was sent to a mission field. He came from a province, a minority and was caught up with the colonial powers and their games. Did he understand that he was part of a colonial mission? Most likely, yes! Could he be considered a martyr from Courland? I would still argue yes.

His name was forgotten in Latvia for at least 85 years, but this research is an attempt to give back his name. Karl Segebrock counted.

References

(1922) Latvijas evaņģeliskās luteriskās baznīcas draudžu mācītāju un priekšstāvju Sinodes sēžu Protokoli. Rīgā, 1922. gadā no 21. līdz 24. februārim, Rīga, Latvijas Lauksaimnieku Centrālbiedrības spiestuve

„Tēvijas Kalendāra" redakcija (1899) 'Kāds vārds par paganu misioni' in Tēvijas Kalendārs 1899. gadam, Rīga, Z. Veinbergs, 5-23

Baznīcas Vēstnesis (1896) 'Ziņas', no. 12, 379-382

Baznīcas Vēstnesis (1897) 'Ziņas', no. 3, 117-121

Baznīcas Vēstnesis (1900) 'Misione', no. 9, 361-364

be. (1936) 'Baltisches Märtyrertum', Rigasche Rundschau, October 10, p. 9

Boettcher, J. (1893) Protokoll der im Jahre 1893 in Mitau abgehaltenen achtundfünfzigsten Kurländischen Provinzial-Synode, Mitau, J. F. Steffenhagen und Sohn

Boettcher, J. (1894) Protokoll der im Jahre 1894 in Mitau abgehaltenen neunundfünfzigsten Kurländischen Provinzial-Synode, Mitau, J. F. Steffenhagen und Sohn

Boettcher, J. (1897) Protokoll der im Jahre 1897 abgehaltenen zwei und sechzigsten Kurländischen

Provinzial- Synode, Mitau, J. F. Steffenhagen und Sohn

Evangelisch-Lutherische Mission zu Leipzig (1895) Vocation for Karl Joseph Segebrock, 8 June, Personalakte von Karl Segebrock, ALMW II/32/412, Franckesche Stiftungen

Feldmanis, Roberts (1942) Protokols Nr. 1. Ārmisijas Referentu Sanāksme 1942. gada 4. novembrī, 1942-43 Misijas referentu sanāksmju protokoli, Roberta Feldmaņa bibliotēkas ārmisijas materiāli

Feldmanis, Roberts (2011) Latvijas baznīcas vēsture, 2nd ed., Rīga, Latvija, Luterisma mantojuma fonds Freibergs, Ernests (1954) 'Kā ārmisiju veicināja Kurzemē', Mājas Draugs, no. 2, p. 8

Grünbergs, Teodors (1932) Latvijas Evaņģēliskās Luteriskās Baznīcas Sinodes protokoli Rīgā VII. (ārkārtējās) - 1931. g. novembrī un VIII. - 1932. g. 29., 30. un 31. martā, Rīga, Valters un Rapa

Katterfeld, Ludwig (1885) ,Diakonie und innere Mission' in Protokoll der am 21. August 1885 in Mitau abgehaltenen fünfzigsten Kurländischen Provinzial-Synode (Jubel-Synode), Mitau, J. F. Steffenhagen und Sohn, 177-203

Katterfeld, Ludwig (1896) Letter to Carl von Schwartz, 9. Dezember, Personalakte von Karl Segebrock, ALMW II/32/412, Franckesche Stiftungen

Lamberg, T. E. (1885) ,Actum Montag den 26. August' in Protokoll der am 21. August 1885 in Mitau abgehaltenen fünfzigsten Kurländischen Provinzial-Synode (Jubel-Synode), Mitau, J. F. Steffenhagen und Sohn, 16-19

Lauciņš, Voldemārs (2015) The Right Man in the Right Place: the Role of Kārlis Irbe (1861-1934) in the Formation and Development of the Evangelical Lutheran Church of Latvia, 1916-1928, Helsinki, University of Helsinki, Faculty of Theology

m. (1896) 'Nonāvēti misionāri', Latviešu Avīzes, October 30, p. 3.

Mühlenbachs, Fricis (1922) 'Iekšlietu ministrija un evaņģ.-luterāņu baznīcas pašvaldība', Brīvā Zeme, 16 February, p. 1

Ovir, Ewald (1896) ,Ein Brief vom 11. October. Inland', Duna Zeitung, November 20, p. 2

Panck, O. (1898) Protokoll der im Jahre 1898 abgehaltenen dreiundsechszigsten Kurländischen Provinzial-Synode, Mitau, J. F. Steffenhagen und Sohn

Panck, O. (1901) Protokoll der im Jahre 1901 abgehaltenen sechsundsechzigsten Kurländischen Provinzial-Synode

Riedel, Robert (1936) ,Baltische Missionszeugen in Ostafrika', Rigasche Post October 18, p. 4

Rozentāls, Linards (2012) 'LELB sinodāli episkopālās iekārtas veidošanās priekšnosacījumi un konteksts', in Lauciņš V. (ed.) Kārlis Irbe 1861-1934: 150 gadu jubilejas konferences materiālu krājums, Rīga, Luterisma mantojuma fonds, 123-140

Ryland, Glen P. (2013) Translating Africa for Germans: The Rhenish Mission in Southwest Africa, 1829 -1936, PhD thesis, Notre Dame, Indiana, University of Notre Dame

Salooja, Ravinder (2021) 'Editorial', Kirche weltweit, no. 3/21, p. 2

Schwartz, Carl von (1897) Karl Segebrock und Ewald Ovir. Zwei früh vollendete Missionare der

Evangelisch-lutherischen Mission zu Leipzig, Leipzig, Selbstverlag der Evangelisch-lutherischen Mission

Segebrock, Karl (1889) Mein Lebenslauf, die Personalakte von Karl Segebrock, ALMW II/32/412, Franckesche Stiftungen

Segebrock, Karl (1895a) Letter to Karl von Schwartz, October 7, Personalakte von Karl Segebrock, ALMW II/32/412, Franckesche Stiftungen

Segebrock, Karl (1895b) Letter to Karl von Schwartz, December 29, Personalakte von Karl Segebrock, ALMW II/32/412, Franckesche Stiftungen

Segebrock, Karl (1897a) 'Von Mombasa zum Kilimanjaro', Duna Zeitung, August 21, p. 1

Segebrock, Karl (1897b) 'Von Mombasa zum Kilimanjaro', Duna Zeitung, August 22, p. 1

Segebrock, Karl (1897c) 'Von Mombasa zum Kilimanjaro', Duna Zeitung, August 27, p. 1

Siedenburg, J. (1896) 'Vermischtes. Riga. 29. October', Goldingenscher Anzeiger, 2. November, p. 2

Svētdienas Rīts (1936) 'Zegebroks un Ovirs', October 25, p. 351

Tēvija (1896) 'Ārzemju ziņas', October 30, p. 3

Weide, I. (1882) 'No iekšzemēm. Kurzemes mācītāju sinode', Latviešu Avīzes, September 22 (October 4), p. 297

Weissmanis, J. (1903) 'Kurzeme. No Zaļeniekiem. Pirmais latviešu tautības misionārs', Latviešu Avīzes, June 6, p. 2.

Wilpert, K. (1856) Protokoll der im Jahre 1856 in Libau gehaltenen einundzwanzigsten Kurländischen Provinzial-Synode, Libau

Karolin Wetjen

Symposium Climbing High Mountains: What we have learned – A commentary

First of all, I would like to thank you for your inspiring and thought-provoking papers and congratulate Ravinder Salooja, Antje Lanzendorf, and Daniel Keiling for organizing this excellent online workshop.

Before delving into the task of summarizing the workshops and identifying points for further discussion, I'd like to offer two minor caveats to clarify my perspective. While my academic focus has been on studying the history of the Leipzig Mission Society, including its mission work in East Africa with attention to theological dimensions, it's important to note that I am a historian, not a theologian. Secondly, I bring a European perspective to the table, having been born, raised, and trained in Germany.

From this point of view, four points seem to be worth considering:

1. Today, we have heard various accounts of what happened on October 19 and 20, 1896. Moritz Fischer and Moni Parisius even presented us with a list of various publications about the incident. However, I would argue that it is crucial to consider the power of narratives and the archive. What has become clear is that the story of the two missionaries who were killed by Ilarusa and became martyrs for the Christian faith is a narrative that effectively played into the colonial and mission propaganda in the German Empire at the time, and even in the 1930s. This narrative should be interpreted within the continuing need to underline and legitimize the colonial civilizing mission. Still, this poses a problem that everyone dealing with mission history faces: Analysing sources in the history of missions requires deep methodological and theoretical reflections. Most mission societies, like the Leipzig Mission, have a comprehensive archive that includes not only written but also material sources and a vast number of pictures. However, these sources are primarily written from a European missionary perspective and require a high degree of tact and methodical tools. How can the voices of those from whom we have little or no written evidence be made audible without concealing the power imbalances? How can we include the silenced Chagga in the history of the killings or the perspective of the Ilarusa?

2. The Akeri killings can illustrate the various entanglements between mission and colonialism. According to Shalini Randeria and Sebastian Conrad, a history of entanglements emphasizes similarities and relationships. However, it also reveals that interactions and entanglements produced not only a shared history but also a divided history full of conflicts and dissonances. This approach underscores the agency of the local people who were mar-

ginalized in the European-centered mission's written record; the perspective on entanglements also clarifies the relationships between the mission spaces and the different actors of the mission organization in the German Empire – or in Latvia, as Kristina Ecis has shown – and the mission field. Missionaries were part of a hierarchically organized mission society, so the society's leadership took part in decisions in the mission field, at least indirectly. Additionally, missionaries were intensely involved in various networks of a broader mission public, actively engaged in discussions on religion in the German public, and contributed to ongoing contemporary debates in the field of theology and especially in the formation of missiology. Considering the different actors, spaces, and networks the missions were part of and include them productively in an analysis of the event, it becomes clear that the reasons and dynamics that culminated in the Akeri killings were indeed complex. Moritz Fischer argued that the missionaries were squeezed between the two armies and that the killings were part of anti-colonial resistance. However, the missionaries were not innocent members of a third party but had proven on other occasions that they were profoundly connected with the German colonial rule and part of a generation of missionaries deeply influenced by and actively shaping the colonial discourse.

3. Ongoing postcolonial discussions in Germany, for example, the broad debate on the colonial heritage of objects in the Humboldt Forum or on the renaming of streets, point to a growing consciousness of the German colonial past that was until recently subject to amnesia or even colonial aphasia. Mission societies need to take an active part in these discussions. That is why I think this workshop was so important.

Ravinder Saaloja yesterday underlined in his introduction that usually only the two missionaries were remembered, although five Chagga were also killed. Additionally, we also need to remember the Arusha who were killed by the German *"Schutztruppe"* as victims of the German colonial rule. Today, Harald Bollermann especially asked how the killed Africans could be included in the memory, which seems a critical point to me.

Furthermore, what we have learned in this workshop is that the killings can be interpreted as a history of German colonialism as well as of church growth in Tanzania. Reverend Majola has underlined this aspect in his paper this morning.

How colonialism is remembered here in Germany is one part of the story, but how the colonial past is remembered and interpreted in the formerly colonized regions is another. Memories of colonialism are essential elements of a 'shared' and 'entangled' colonial history. The papers in this workshop stressed how the killings were part of a shared history. However, throughout the workshop, I wondered if this shared mission history is really the whole story and whether the experiences of the colonized at the time were indeed rather differently from these current interpretations. In short, the notion of a shared history must not be used to gloss over the past.

4. My fourth point concerns the consequences for future missions. What has become clear to me and what has been stressed by postcolonial theologians like Jörg Rieger is that mission is

no longer practicable in the traditional sense. Konstantin Gerber mentioned the painful path to giving up the claim to universality, although we know that this claim is deeply inscribed in the Christian mission. Mission in the nineteenth and twentieth century as well as now needs to be understood as a process, a dynamic, and a relationship that is not taking place in a political vacuum. Instead, mission today is still embedded in various power-relations that we need to be aware of. Even though colonialism, in its political manifestations of direct government over a particular area, seems to be over, many of the colonial structures persist and continue at other levels, including the economic and the intellectual. Hence, theology is asked to reflect (even more) on its colonial history and its epistemic violence. Gladson Jathanna showed that how mission and conversion are perceived depends on the political sphere in the post-colonial world and how conversion is deeply embedded in power relations. He argued that conversion goes beyond the colonial space and that conversion also opened up possibilities for resistance. Thereby, he stressed the independent agency of the converted Keeping that in mind is crucial whenever the future of mission is discussed in the subaltern perspective. I strongly feel, what is needed is a true dialogue that reflects upon power-inequalities and in which the Europeans mainly listen.

References/further readings

Conrad, Sebastian/Shalini Randeria (2002) Einleitung. Geteilte Geschichten – Europa in einer post-kolonialen Welt, in: Dies. (Hg.), Jenseits des Eurozentrismus, Frankfurt a. M./New York: Campus Verlag, 9-49.

Habermas, Rebekka, Restitutionsdebatten, Koloniale Aphasie und die Frage, was Europa ausmacht in: Apuz 40 (2019), 17-22.

Habermas, Rebekka/Richard Hölzl (2014) Mission global. Eine Verflechtungsgeschichte seit dem 19. Jahrhundert, Köln/Weimar/Wien: Böhlau

Ratschiller, Linda/Karolin Wetjen (2018) Verflochtene Mission. Ansätze, Methoden und Fragestellungen einer neuen Missionsgeschichte, in: Dies. (Hg.), Verflochtene Mission. Perspektiven auf eine neue Missionsgeschichte, Köln/Weimar/Wien: Böhlau, 9-24.

Rieger, Joerg (2004) Theology and Mission Between Neocolonialism and Postcolonialism, in: Mission Studies 21, 201-227.

Stoler, Ann Laura (2016) Duress. Imperial Durabilities in Our Times, Durham: Duke University Press

Wetjen, Karolin (2020) Mission als theologisches Labor. Koloniale Aushandlungen des Religiösen in Ostafrika, Stuttgart: Franz Steiner Verlag

The following contribution is based on a lecture held at the conference "Colonial Violence: Secular and Ecclesiastical Perspectives (1919-1975)" in Praia, Cape Verde. The conference gathered scholars from different disciplines to study the phenomenon of colonial violence.

Ravinder Salooja

Mission Justifying Colonial Violence

The 1936 publication of *Evangelisch-Lutherische Missionsgesellschaft Leipzig* (Leipzig Evangelical Lutheran Mission Society; henceforth: LELMS[1]) *"Blutzeugen am Meru"* ("Blood martyrs at Mt. Meru") (Müller, 1936) relates to the death of seven mission workers in the night of October 20, 1896 (Handmann, 1896b) at the slopes of Mt. Meru in Tanganyika, West of Mt. Kilimanjaro. Among the victims were two Baltic missionaries sent there by LELMS, who are in the focus of this 1936 publication. Eleven days later, from October 31, 1896 onward, the German colonial administration through its *Deutsche Schutztruppe* fought a three week retaliation war against the involved local Ilarusha and Wameru people (Handmann, 1896a: 471; Handmann, 1897d: 52; Handmann, 1897b: 57; Handmann, 1897c, p. This essay presents the assessment of the 1936 publication *"Blutzeugen am Meru"* on this act of colonial violence.

1. Questions, method, and relevance of the research

My research questions were: 1. How did Leipzig Evangelical Lutheran Mission Society assessed the retaliation war of the *Deutsche Schutztruppe*? 2. Can this assessment be perceived as justifying the act of colonial violence towards the Ilarusha and Wameru people? To answer these questions, I used the method of critical discourse analysis with focus on the 1936 publication as the last LELMS publication on the 1896 event[2].

Around the centenary of the Versailles Treaty in 2019, Protestant mission circles in Germany discussed the issue of "mission and colonialism". The way this happened indicates the relevance of the research presented in this essay: The main thread of the discussion followed the statement "the missionaries wanted to do good", adding the line "they also helped col-

---

[1]   Over time various English translations were used to name the historic *"Evangelisch-Lutherische Missions-gesellschaft Leipzig"* ("Leipzig Evangelical Lutheran Mission Society"). The handy abbreviation LMS is generally used for the London Missionary Society. Therefore, in this paper I am using the unusual acronym LELMS for the historic mission society, which for the better includes the decisive terms "Leipzig" and "Lutheran". Today's successor organization *"Evangelisch-Lutherisches Missionswerk Leipzig"*, in short also *"Leipziger Missionswerk"*, in English for convenience is often abbreviated as "Leipzig Mission", since the addition *"werk"* is a typical German word resisting translation.

[2]   Parisius (2024) mentions a 1946 post-war unprinted poem of Pastor Ranft which he assumed was recited in a liturgical context, followed by an "epoch of silence". What Parisius calls "the postcolonial era" began with Parsalaw (1999) (cf. Parsalaw, 2000) as the first to resume the narration of the death of LELMS' seven missionaries, but with a different perspective. Likewise, Altena (2003) examines the 1896 nightly deaths with a critical approach.

onized people against the colonial system". As part of this approach the concept of "Third Space" which originates in historical science was used legitimizing this re-lecture of mission history (Knuth, 2022). Inserted into the frame "the German colonialism lasted only a very short time" a lack of responsibility towards the involvement of one's own predecessors becomes apparent. Those successor mission agencies that are internationalized, i.e. being part of an international network of missions and churches[3], tend to proclaim "this is not our discussion, because we are 'beyond', as our worldwide stakeholders in majority are representing the formerly colonized people".

2. Leipzig Evangelical Lutheran Mission Society as the organizational context

Leipzig Evangelical Lutheran Mission Society (LELMS) was founded in 1836 as the first confessional Lutheran mission society, hereafter receiving overwhelmingly support from mission minded circles in Lutheran church territories all over Europe. The operative work began in 1839 in South Australia (lasting till 1846), followed by Tamil Nadu (India) in 1840, which then became the "heartland" of LELMS. German East Africa was taken as mission field in 1893, followed 1953 by Papua New Guinea (as well as for a short time from 1953 onward Brazil, serving German migrants there, as it was done in the 19th century in North America two years, too) (Fleisch, 1936; Moritzen, 1986; Salooja, 2018b)[4].

Sending missionaries to German East Africa was a late decision, taken in 1892 after a change in LELMS' management 1891 (Günther, 1992). In the years before, LELMS' governing board hesitated towards working in a colonial territory linked with one's own nation. A major consideration was, whether it will support the mission agenda or not (Salooja, 2018a: 82; cf. Salooja, 2022a: 65). But anyhow, from the beginning LELMS had already been operating within the context of colonialism, be it in South Australia, be it in Tamil Nadu. Specifically concerning German East Africa, LELMS commenced work in the Kilimanjaro region in 1893 only after the border disputes between Germany and Britain had been settled, which made the Kilimanjaro region part of the German colony. The first five LELMS missionaries were sent to Kilimanjaro in 1893, among them Emil Müller, the author of the 1936 *"Blutzeugen am Meru"*. LELMS' operation in Tanganyika paused during World War I and due to the Versailles Treaty, was resumed in 1925, and again was paused in World War II (Fleisch, 1936; Moritzen, 1986).

3. Research method and material

Starting from textual patterns, a critical discourse analysis (Jäger, 2015) seeks to access mental and social patterns, and thus trace and disclose discourse patterns. As these are embedded

---

3   E.g. United Evangelical Mission (UEM) as succeeding the Rhenish Missionary Society; Evangelical Mission in Solidarity (EMS), partly succeeding the German parts of the Basel Mission Society.

4   The origin of the LELMS is a Mission Auxiliary Association founded 1819 in Dresden supporting the Basel Mission. In 1936 this association was turned into the independent "Ev.-Luth. Missionsgesellschaft zu Dresden in Sachsen", which received it's final name "Ev.-Luth. Missionsgesellschaft Leipzig" after its relocation to Leipzig in 1848.

into texts (as part of civilization) and mentality (with codes and knowledge, that are activated through texts) they have their effects through being shared by individuals and institutions (Siefkes, 2013). Accordingly, a critical discourse analysis is a suitable research method for the given task finding out whether and how LELMS justified an act of colonial violence.

The 1936 publication "*Blutzeugen am Meru*" is the last independent, monograph publication by LELMS on the event after a series of other monographs beginning as early as 1897 relating partly or extensively on the event (Schwartz, 1897; Adolphi, 1902; Schanz and Adolphi, 1912; Weishaupt, 1913; Weishaupt, 1916, 1925; cf. Parisius, 2024). The first notes and reports were given in LELMS' periodical *Evangelisch-Lutherisches Missionsblatt* of 1896 and 1897 (Handmann, 1896a; Handmann, 1896b; Handmann, 1897a; Handmann, 1897b; Handmann, 1897c; and Handmann, 1897d). "*Blutzeugen am Meru*" was published towards the 40th commemoration of the 1896 event. But the year of publication was most probably chosen due to the centenary of LELMS (Salooja, 2022a: 64), which was celebrated for several days in August 1936 beginning with a big public event on the central marketplace in Leipzig (Salooja, 2022b).

4. Defining "the event" as an act of colonial violence

In the night of October 20, 1896 two missionaries – Ewald Ovir and Karl Segebrock – together with five local mission workers – Mrio, Karava, Kalami and two others, whose names are still to be retraced – encountered death in a nightly attack in the course of extending LELMS' mission work from Mt. Kilimanjaro to Mt. Meru. A squadron of the *Deutsche Schutztruppe* under Captain Johannes was "witness" to this in several ways: Earlier that day the German military squadron witnessed the purchase of the mission areal from Wameru chief Matunda, as the acquisition took place in the military camp that had been erected roughly one kilometer away from the mission camp. Secondly, in the night the squadron witnessed the attack as it was attacked, too (and might have even been the primary target); the squadron could successfully repel the attackers. After the repulse the German soldiers became ear witnesses of the attack on the mission camp. Thirdly, in the morning they discovered and buried the bodies of the Baltic missionaries. They also took care of the bodies of the locals.[5]

As a retaliation war, October 31, 1896 the *Deutsche Schutztruppe* began a three week raid against the involved Ilarusha and Wameru people at Mt. Meru, killing several hundred men, expelling women and children, confiscating cattle and livestock, destroying the fruit fields (banana plants) of the local people, and finally gave the land to German and other colonial settlers (Mesaki, 2013; cf. Handmann, 1896a: 471; Handmann, 1897d: 52; Handmann, 1897b: 57; Handmann, 1897c: 120).

This retaliation war is "the event" debated, and it is the assessment of this event of colonial violence in the LELMS publications that is under research in the discourse analysis.

---

5   Parsalaw (1999) named this nightly attack event „Akeri killings", regarding the place Akeri where it happened. In his important research he presents detailed considerations based on local resources concerning the reasons for the attack as well as insights into the aftermath of the retaliation war of the *Deutsche Schutztruppe*.

5. Research results

5.1 Naming "the event"

Emil Müller in his *"Blutzeugen am Meru"* (1936) narrates the retaliation war as follows:

> *"10,000 Chagga auxiliary warriors with their chiefs joined the reinforced Schutztruppe on Saturday, October 31, during a terrible thunderstorm in the steppe. The invasion of the well-defended Meru land could only be forced through hard fighting; there was no lack of setbacks. The war, which was given the name 'Rain War' because of the particularly heavy rainy season of that year, ended with the defeat of the Arusha and Meru people and their punishment by taking about 6000 head of cattle and countless goats and sheep, which now form the basis of the new cattle breeding on Kilimanjaro." (Müller, 1936, 20f; own translation).*

In this 1936 publication for the first time "rain war" (*"Regen-Krieg"*) is mentioned as the name of the event. By this, the event is titled as "war"[6]. Other early word used were "punishment" (Handmann, 1896a: 471), "punitive expedition" (Handmann, 1897b: 57; Handmann, 1897c: 120), "castigation" (Handmann, 1897a: 19) and "battle" (Handmann, 1896a: 471). But then, the "adversaries" in the war – the men killed as well as the expelled women and children – are not mentioned at all.

The first longer description of the event was published already in 1897 as "The bloody baptism of our mission at Mt. Meru" (*"Die Bluttaufe unserer Mission am Meru"*) in LELMS' periodical by the editor Handmann (Handmann, 1897a). Here the period of reporting is extended to the previous year 1895: "After Captain Johannes chastised the residents of Arusha in October 1895 for attacking the Meru people, we believed that peace and security now reigned on the Meru." (Handmann, 1897a: 12; own translation).

In contrast, in the very first independent publication "Karl Segebrock und Ewald Ovir" (Schwartz, 1897) later in 1897 by LELMS Director Karl von Schwartz, the retaliation raid and war of the colonial *Deutsche Schutztruppe* is not mentioned at all, though it was already named before in the periodical.

In his 1936 publication Müller also mentions the use of the confiscated cattle for colonial production means. This alludes to the colonial allocation of the land to settlers from South Africa in the course of the consolidation of German colonial rule, with consequences far into the presence (Mesaki, 2013: 17).

5.2 Naming the "opponents"

As stated above, in the description of the colonial retaliation war of the *Deutsche Schutztruppe* the local people dying are not mentioned. By only summing them up under "the defeat of the Arusha and Meru people" (Müller, 1936: 21; own translation), they are part of the abstract noun "the defeat", and therefore are even not considered as persons. This is in

---

6   This word is used for the first time in 1897 as „war of punishment", cf. Handmann, 1897d: 52.

contrast with the naming and nomination
- of the attackers of the night of October 20, 1896 as "predatory" ("*räuberisch*") (Hand-mann, 1896b: 433) "murderers" ("*Mörder*") (Handmann, 1896b: 433; Handmann, 1896a: 471; Handmann, 1897a: 18; Handmann, 1897b: 57; Schwartz, 1897: 2) and "gang" ("*Rotte*") (Handmann, 1897a: 18; Handmann, 1897d: 51), motivated by "rapacity, lust for murder, hatred" ("*die Raubgier, die Mordlust, der Haß*") (Schwartz, 1897: 1);
- of the death of the Leipzig missionaries as "murder" ("*Mord*") (Müller, 1936, 3; 17; 19; cf. as early as 1896: Handmann, 1896b: 433; Handmann, 1897d: 51; Schwartz, 1897, 1, 95[7]), but also as "sacrifice" ("*Opfer*") (Müller, 1936: 20; cf. Handmann, 1896b: 433), as well as the missionaries as "blood martyrs of Christ" ("*Blutzeugen Christi*") (Schwartz, 1897, 1f); Handmann in the first 1897 narration uses words like "sudden and violent death" ("*jähen und gewaltsamen Tod*"), "bloody end of the brothers" ("*blutiges Ende der Brüder*"), and "calamity on [Mt.] Meru" ("*Unglück am Meru*") (Handmann, 1897a, 12);
- of the nightly attack on the seven Mission workers as "ambush" ("*Überfall*") (Müller, 1936, 3; 18; cf. already Handmann, 1897b: 57) and "bloody deed" ("*Bluttat*") (Müller, 1936: 4).

This is all the more clear in contrast to the local people fighting on the side of the Germans, as they are narrated as "10.000 Chagga auxiliary warriors with their chiefs" (Müller, 1936: 20; own translation).

5.3 Assessment of colonial rule

Following the description of the retaliation war, Müller's narration covers the following years:

> "*So peace was made, but not kept [...] The Meru, and with it the Kilimanjaro [area], never came to rest. Again and again, campaigns of war were necessary, which brutalized the Chagga men in particular; for the only effective discipline for Meru was the robbing of cattle and women. Nevertheless, it happened that in December 1899 an attempt was made to attack the military station [Moschi], and even chiefs of the Chagga were involved in the conspiracy. Not even the executions of March 1, 1900, and the burning down of the homes of the guilty brought peace [...] At that point, we Leipzig missionaries felt that securing Mount Meru with a military station in Arusha was the only way to finally bring about peace. This serious measure has actually put an end to robbery and murder in the whole area and dampened the arrogance of the Arusha people in particular. There was peace!*" (Müller, 1936: 21; own translation).

Müller's narration of the situation and events of the years to follow till 1900 shows that for the LELMS missionaries only colonial rule with its administration and through its military force established a situation for them to work and live, which they called "peace". This comes in line with the book praising the stabilizing effect of the German colonial regime as well as its civilizing "cultural" mission successes:

---

7   Handmann (1897a: 17) used this word in a quotation from Captain Johannes.

> *"Peace had been established by the strong arm of the German Reich, most of the Chagga states and tribes conformed to the new order, indeed some, like the great Madjame in the west, were heartily glad and grateful that they were no longer oppressed by hostile neighbors; even Maasailand was of little concern. The first fine veins of European achievements began to run through what was newly annexed: truly straight paths and not just the caravan 'roads', stretching straight enough for two feet next to each other, sometimes winding with, often without a reason, that connected countries and lands; mail no longer took six weeks or more from Germany to the hands of its recipients; Greek and Indian shops opened to offer salt and sugar, clothing and jewelry to the natives; handy blank silver and copper coins were to gradually replace the expensive and cumbersome barter goods." (Müller, 1936: 3; own translation).*

Müller here combines colonial rule with the achievements of civilizing mission. He additionally mentions that the establishment of local peace through colonial rule was welcomed by the local people, too, hereby suggesting the colonized people favored colonial rule. Accordingly, the colonial context of LELMS' mission work is described to the readers in a way, to which they were able to positively connect.

At the beginning, *"Blutzeugen am Meru"* concedes that colonial rule needed time to be established, and the mission work at Mt. Meru as well as the death of the mission workers in 1896 are being seen in the broader context of colonial German East Africa:

> *"Europeanism, with its systematic approach and equipment, had only overrun the East African tribes in their isolation and fragmentation, who were holding simple weapons intended only for close combat between men, so that the actual decision had yet to be made. For these N[****] tribes, experience came with time, and with it came reflection, and often disappointment, and both justified and unfounded fears. Weak tribes chose blunt, dull, hopeless submission, while relatively healthy, warlike tribes chose to fight at the opportune time, as soon as a watchword was found that could guide everything else. It was the same on Meru, and the mission, which had good reasons to go with the new times, also had to have a share in their destiny." (Müller, 1936: 4; own translation).*

This quote serves to support the notion to the readers that establishing the "advanced", European colonial reign demanded sacrifices, to which in the end mission had to contribute, too. In line of the European civilizing mission, in which LELMS' mission was considered to participate, the death of the mission workers would have to be seen as unavoidable, whereas the local victims of colonial military domination did not matter. Likewise, the 1936 publication in its introduction states:

> *"The missionaries, few in number, were not at all blind to the fact that all this and many other modest advances would also help them to pursue their goal of proclaiming the Good News of Jesus Christ to all these N[****] tribes sooner and more easily. External pacification should be followed by internal pacification." (Müller, 1936: 3; own translation).*

As an intermediate result it can be concluded that the 1936 book presents colonial rule as a necessary, positive framework for missionary work.

In the 1902 publication *"Am Fuße der Bergriesen Ostafrikas"* ("At the foot of the mountain giants of East Africa") by H. Adolphi the retaliation war of November 1896 as well as the 1899/1900 "ultimate" wars of the *Deutsche Schutztruppe* in the Greater Kilimanjaro region are narrated in more explicit details. It approves them as

"The secular authorities had to act in this way in order to keep order in the country and to protect the reputation of the government." (Adolphi, 1902: 58; own translation; similarly already Handmann, 1897a: 19),

and

> *"Even if [...] [the attempt of 1899 to conquer Moshi military station] was unsuccessful, the punishment could not be missed. Shortly after his return, therefore, Captain Johannes undertook a war campaign against the rebels." (Adolphi, 1902: 109; own translation).*

But in contrast to other references, the retaliation war of November 1896 in the 1902 publication is just mentioned as "in this way", and the wars of 1899/1900 are titled as "campaign".

5.4 Addressees

A discourse analysis tries to relate the findings to the audience, since trough text patterns it intends to access mental and social patterns. Therefore, it is now attempted to sketch some aspects of the addressees of the publication.

The 1896/97 short notices in LELMS' periodical *"Evangelisch-Lutherisches Missionsblatt"* were read by mission minded groups, mission theologians as well as supporters subscribing to the periodical. The 1902 book of H. Adolphi *"Am Fuße der Bergriesen Ostafrikas"* (Adolphi, 1902, published in a second, revised edition by J. Schanz in 1912) with its colored frontpage gives a good impression of how it was meant to attract attention of a wider, public audience. Generally, the independent monograph publications were to be sold to a wide audience not accessible through the mission periodicals. These monographs contain photographs and maps, and partly explain specific terms not known to a general, uninformed reader, e.g. the term "Askari".

Contrasted with a contemporary edition of Karl May's widely read "Winnetou" stories about a German traveler becoming the blood brother of a native American, telling all his "true" life stories to the German reader of the outgoing 19th century reveals a surprising similarity. A closer textual comparison might even reveal more intentions of LELMS' monograph publications as well as influences of each other. But that is beyond the scope of this essay.

The 1936 publication in our focus, however, just has a simple black and white, but nevertheless manifold cover, with varying titles and photographs offering the reader a range of impressions before having even read one word.

The cover page titles *"Blutzeugen am Meru"* and is decorated with a picture of the gr ave of the two Baltic missionaries. Inside a new, second title page is included, giving the title *"Aus der Tiefe in die Höh'"* ("From the depths up to the heights"). Then follows "20. Oktober 1896 – 1936", indicating the time from the death of the missionaries until the publication of the book, and afterwards the explanation *"Segebrock und Ovir, unsere Blutzeugen am Meru"*; again, the five local mission workers who died, too, are not mentioned here. Finally, the au-

H. Adolphi, Am Fuße der Bergriesen Ostafrikas (1902)

Karl May, Winnetou (1893)

Müller (1936), front page

Müller (1936), inside title page

Müller (1936), backside (left) of inside title page

thor "Emil Müller" is mentioned, with the explanation "formerly missionary in East Africa" ("*früher Missionar in Ostafrika*"). The next page left side presents the pictures and names of Karl Segebrock and Ewald Ovir.

5.5 Content of the 1936 publication

The greatest part of the 1936 publication is filled with the life of the two missionaries, from their Baltic homes to joining LELMS' missionary training seminar at Leipzig, their personality, up to their arrival and work in Tanganyika within the development of LELMS there. In essence, the 1936 book provides the reader with the success story of LELMS mission work at Kilimanjaro as well as Meru. The "Akeri killings" with the death of Ovir and Segebrock as well as the retaliation war is presented as part of that success story.

5.6 Guarantee of authenticity

The front page of the 1936 publication states that the author Emil Müller had himself been a missionary in German East Africa. As member of the first group of Leipzig missionaries at Mt. Kilimanjaro in Tanganyika in 1893, he became the head of LELMS' very first East African mission station Machame, from where Ovir, Segebrock, and the five local missionaries set out west towards Mt. Meru in 1896. Müller then was among the first to receive news on the death of the seven Leipzig workers. In the days to come, he was a contemporary witness of the retaliation war, too.

Müller presents a good acquaintance and personal relationship with the two missionaries Ewald Ovir and Karl Segebrock, on whom the book is focusing:

> "*I knew Segebrock from four years of joint seminary life (1889-93) in Leipzig, and from autumn 1895 in East Africa; Ovir until [my] own commissioning as my roommate [in Leipzig], and from autumn 1895 until his appointment to Meru as a learning colleague in Madjame.*" (Müller, 1936: 5; own translation).

This information is to guarantee a kind of authenticity of the story told and are meant to assure the reader about the truth told in the book. Accordingly, the whole story and every part of it told in the 1936 publication are to be accepted by the reader as "true".

6. Assembling the research results

Throughout LELMS' publications, there is a consistent line in naming the local people connected with the 1896 nightly attack, the attack itself as well as the 1896 October-November retaliation war ("the event" under research). From the very beginning, the death of the seven missionaries, was named "murder", while the retaliation war of the *Deutsche Schutztruppe* was presented as a "necessary" "punitive" "campaign." Due to the character of short notices, the 1896/1897 references in the periodical are not as lengthy as in the following independent publications.

In the publications generally informing about LELMS' work in German East Africa, the nightly death of the mission workers as well as the 1896 October-November retaliation war are presented as part of LELMS' mission work. But in the 1936 book the retaliation war of

1896 against the Ilarusa and Wameru people is mentioned less detailed than in earlier publications. It recedes to the background of the story told.

With the wider circle of German speaking readers in mind, the 1936 publication might have been intended to create further support for the work of LELMS, and accordingly it would understandably present LELMS' mission commitment as well developed and as success. As the booklet was published along with or shortly after the centenary celebration, where several thousands of mission minded supporters came with special buses and trains from afar joining the fête, this is a reasonable consideration. This might be supported by the second title page of the 1936 publication heading "*Aus der Tiefe in die Höh'*" ("From the depth up to high"), which alludes to a known religious song "*Aus der Enge in die Weite, aus der Tiefe in die Höh'*" (*Liederkranz für Sonntags-Schulen und Jugend-Vereine*, 1898: 202; music by S. Zeller, the lyrics was composed by Friedrich Wilhelm Kniepkamp[8] (1859-1936); cf. Jehle, 1918a, Jehle, 1918b) known in Germany even outside missionary contexts until the 1970s (Zilz, 1927; Kaul, 1952; Wollmershäuser, 1972; Niederstein, 1978).

Considering the possibly intended audience, there is another observation concerning a specific term used describing the 1896 November retaliation war on the Ilarusa and Wameru throughout all the publications, i.e. the word "punishment" in "punishment raid" ("*Strafzug*"), "punitive campaign" ("*Strafexpedition*"), "punishment" ("*Bestrafung*"), and "not to be left unpunished" ("*nicht unbestraft bleiben*") (cf. references above). In German language these terms at least in some constellations come close to "castigation" and "caning". Apart from the direct meaning, they also appeal to a 19th (and even 20th) century European pedagogic framework where punishment resp. castigation was seen as an integral part of learning of those who need to learn: misbehaving pupils, and stubborn people, for whom you took responsibility.

This observation has two significant aspects. First: Both LELMS and the missionaries appealed to the shared mental framework of their German (and European) context, including its educational and pedagogic concepts. Whatever they wrote and how the assessed the 1896 event, they could confidently base it on being in line with the overall cultural values in their contemporary German context. Second: The missionaries as well as LELMS considered the military actions of the *Deutsche Schutztruppe* purely as an educational and pedagogic issue, just as non-conforming pupils need to be educated.

Accordingly, one main message in the discourse pattern concerning the retaliation war of the *Deutsche Schutztruppe* – and as part of that the case of the deceased seven mission workers – was: We, LELMS, acted in line with what is right and correct in your eyes, too; there is no fault on our side, we did no wrong; as part of educating the local people in Tanganyika, the "punishment" was a necessity[9]. Therefore, there was no reason to expect other than a

---

8   In Wuppertal, where also the Rhenische Missionary Society was located, Kniekamp founded a singing association. The song „Aus der Enge in die Weite, aus der Tiefe in die Höh'" was published abroad, e.g. in a songbook used for sunday schools and youth clubs in Northern America in St. Louis 1898.

9   This interpretation of the message is also supported by several notes in all of the publications: From that the setup of the new Meru Mission station was planned and coordinated with the Foreign office in Germany as well as the local colonial authorities, down to the narrative piece that the purchase of the new Mission territory

successful station building, and as the nightly attack came seemingly out of nowhere, it was even more despicable.

7. Mission justifying colonial violence

How did Leipzig Mission assess the retaliation war of the *Deutsche Schutztruppe* of 1896, which undoubtedly was an act of colonial violence towards the Ilarusa and Wameru people? And can this assessment be understood as justifying this act of colonial violence?

1. Leipzig Evangelical Lutheran Mission Society judged the retaliation war of the *Deutsche Schutztruppe* against the Ilarusa and Wameru people with its violence as an action in no way questionable, but rather reasonable.
2. The Ilarusa and Wameru victims of the retaliation war – warriors as well as expelled civilians – are not narrated as persons but are rather subsumed under abstract words. Likewise, the attack and the attackers of the October 20, 1896 nightly Akeri killings are designated with negative terms. In contrary, the victims among LELMS' mission workers as well as the warriors fighting with the *Deutsche Schutztruppe* are presented as persons and individuals.
3. By placing the narration of the 1896 event into the general German educational and pedagogical framework, it was understood as a necessary and even welcomed action teaching those who have to be taught.
4. The idea of necessity is also supported by the notion of restoring and maintaining local colonial order and rule as a good civilizing mission, that eradicated warfare among local people, brought upon peace to the context, and led to economic and modern development of the region.
5. As the discourse pattern developed in time, the retaliation war of 1896 is described less detailed, and by this rather recedes into the background of the overall narration.
6. One last aspect: Prior to Müller citing the retaliation as "rain war", he quotes from a letter he had received from his missionary colleague Gerhard Althaus from neighboring Mamba mission station, like Müller one of the first five LELMS missionaries:

> *"Thinking of what must now follow, Althaus wrote to me on October 23: I would be happy, very happy indeed, to express myself to you, dear brother; I can't do it in writing. I only want to say that it is a dreadful thought to me that the messengers of peace should be avenged in such a ghastly, bloody way ... But I can see that there is no other way."* (Müller, 1936: 20; own translation).

Althaus' letter was dated three days after the death of the seven LELMS workers, and eight days prior to the beginning of the retaliation war of the *Deutsche Schutztruppe*. Obviously Althaus (and possibly all the other LELMS missionaries at Kilimanjaro) was quite aware that the action of the *Deutsche Schutztruppe*, even though not requested for by the missionaries,

---

at Mt. Meru was done in the military camp, under the eyes of the German military chief Hauptmann Johannes, and that even though he had asked the missionaries to stay overnight neither Hauptmann Johannes nor the missionaries anticipated the nightly attack.

was going be an act of severe violence. Althaus saw a contradiction against the peace message of the Gospel the missionaries were proclaiming. Nevertheless, also here, or rather: already here, even before the act of violence happened, the notion of necessity of the upcoming war ultimately kept the upper hand.

The discourse pattern on the retaliation war of *Deutsche Schutztruppe* as an act of colonial violence against the Ilarusa and Wameru people brought to light in LELMS' publications up to the 1936 book *"Blutzeugen am Meru"* clearly shows a justification of this act of colonial violence. Accordingly, the question whether mission justified colonial violence can be affirmed.

LELMS among 19th century German and European mission societies generally took a middle position on colonial involvement: Neither was LELMS among the strong supporters of a colonial mission (unlike the well-known pro-colonial Friedrich Fabri of Rhenish Missionary Society), nor was LELMS among the strong opponents (like Franz Michael Zahn from North German Missionary Society). Accordingly, it can be assumed that the general justification of colonial violence, which is clearly evident in the elaborated discourse pattern, has to be taken for granted generally for other German mission societies of that time, too.

References

Adolphi, Heinrich. (1902) Am Fuße der Bergriesen Ostafrikas: Geschichte der Leipziger Evangelisch-lutherischen Mission in Deutsch-Ostafrika, Leipzig

Altena, Torsten (2003) "Ein Häuflein Christen mitten in der Heidenwelt des dunklen Erdteils": Zum Selbst- und Fremdverständnis protestantischer Missionare im kolonialen Afrika 1884 - 1918, Münster

Fleisch, Paul (1936) Hundert Jahre lutherischer Mission, Leipzig

Günther, Jürgen (1992) Karl von Schwartz und die Mission der Leipziger Mission in Ostafrika während der deutschen Kolonialzeit: Ein Braunschweiger Beitrag zur Weltmission, Wissenschaftliche Hausarbeit zur Zweiten Theologischen Prüfung, Ev.-luth. Landeskirche in Braunschweig

Handmann, Richard (1896a) 'Missionschronik', Evangelisch-Lutherisches Missionsblatt, no. 22, 470–471

Handmann, Richard (1896b) 'Trauerbotschaft aus Ostafrika', Evangelisch-Lutherisches Missionsblatt, no. 22, 433–436

Handmann, Richard (1897a) 'Die Bluttaufe unserer Mission am Meru: Nach Briefen von Miss. Müller und Faßmann, Evangelisch-Lutherisches Missionsblatt, no. 1, 12–19

Handmann, Richard (1897b) 'Missionschronik', Evangelisch-Lutherisches Missionsblatt, no. 3, 56–57

Handmann, Richard (1897c) 'Missionschronik', Evangelisch-Lutherisches Missionsblatt, no. 6, 119–120

Handmann, Richard (1897d) 'Nachrichten von der Station Moschi', Evangelisch-Lutherisches Missionsblatt, no. 3, 48–54

Jäger, Siegfried (2015) Kritische Diskursanalyse: Eine Einführung, 7th edn, Münster

Jehle, Friedrich (1918a) 'Aus der Enge in die Weite', Monatsschrift für Gottesdienst und kirchliche Kunst, vol. 23, no. 7, p. 169

Jehle, Friedrich (1918b) 'Aus der Enge in die Weite', Monatsschrift für Gottesdienst und kirchliche Kunst, vol. 23, 10/11, p. 249

Kaul, Theodor (ed) (1952) Aus der Enge in die Weite: Beiträge zur Geschichte der Kirche und ihres Volkstums (Georg Biundo von Fachgenossen und Freunden zum 60. Geburtstag dargeboten), Grünstadt

Knuth, Anton (2022) 'War christliche Mission eine andere Form des Kolonialismus? Gedanken zu einer Aushandlungsgeschichte', Deutsches Pfarrerblatt, vol. 122, no. 2, 92–95

(1898) Liederkranz für Sonntags-Schulen und Jugend-Vereine, St. Louis

Mesaki, Simeon (2013) 'Recapping the Meru Land Case, Tanzania', Global Journal of Human Social Sciences. Economics, vol. 13, no. 1, 15–23

Moritzen, Niels-Peter (1986) Werkzeug Gottes in der Welt: Leipziger Mission 1836 - 1936 -1986, Erlangen

Müller, Emil (1936) Blutzeugen am Meru: Aus der Tiefe in die Höh'. 20. Okt. 1896-1936. Segebrock und Ovir, unsere Blutzeugen am Meru. (Von Pfarrer E. Müller, früher Missionar in Ostafrika), Leipzig

Niederstein, Peter (1978) 'Aus der Enge in die Weite', Deutsches Pfarrerblatt, vol. 78, no. 1, 2–5

Parisius, Moni (2024) '125 years of contested memory: A Discourse Analysis of the Reception of the Killings of two Leipzig Missionaries from a Postcolonial Perspective', in this volume

Parsalaw, Joseph W. (1999) A history of the Lutheran Church, Diocese in the Arusha region from 1904 to 1958. (Zugl.: Erlangen, Nürnberg, Univ., Diss., 1997), Erlangen

Parsalaw, Joseph W. (2000) 'The Founding of Arusha Town', in van der Heyden, U. and Stoecker, H. (eds) Mission und Gewalt: Der Umgang christlicher Missionen mit Gewalt und die Ausbreitung des Christentums in Afrika und Asien in der Zeit von 1792 bis 1918/19, Stuttgart, 489–493.

Salooja, Ravinder (2018a) 'Arusha und die Evangelisch-Lutherische Mission zu Leipzig', in EMW - Evangelisches Missionswerk Deutschland e.V. (ed) Vom Geist bewegt - zu verwandelnder Nachfolge berufen: Zur Weltmissionskonferenz in Tansania, Hamburg, 82–87

Salooja, Ravinder (2018b) 'Wechselwirkungen zwischen Sachsen und Genf: Der Beitrag der Leipziger Mission zur Formierung des weltweiten Luthertums', in Evangelisch-Lutherisches Landeskirchenamt Sachsens (ed) Verkündigung durch Begegnung: Kirche sein, leiten und prägen, Dresden, 51–63

Salooja, Ravinder (2022a) 'Climbing High Mountains: Reflexionen über Mission und Kolonialismus mit Bezug auf ein Ereignis in Tanganjika 1896 im Kontext der Arbeit der Leipziger Missionsgesellschaft', in Missionsakademie an der Universität Hamburg (ed) Mission, Kolonialismus, Partnerschaft: Beiträge zu einer postkolonialen Relektüre, Hamburg, 54-69

Salooja, Ravinder (2022b) Jesus ist König: Schriftliche Fassung eines Beitrags zur Jahrestagung der Deutschen Gesellschaft für Missionswissenschaft 2021 zu "Mission & Nationalsozialismus" über die 100-Jahr-Feier der Leipziger Missionsgesellschaft 1936 [Online], Leipzig. Available at http://www.bpm-s.de/ueber-mich/bibliografie.html (Accessed 2 February 2023)

Schanz, Johannes and Adolphi, Heinrich (1912) Am Fuße der Bergriesen Ostafrikas: Geschichte der Leipziger Mission am Kilimandjaro und in den Nachbargebirgen, Leipzig

Schwartz, Karl von (1897) Karl Segebrock und Ewald Ovir: Zwei früh vollendete Missionare der Evangelisch-lutherischen Mission zu Leipzig, Leipzig

Siefkes, Martin (2013) 'Wie wir die Zusammenhänge von Texten, Denken und Gesellschaft verstehen: Ein semiotisches 4-Ebenen-Modell der Diskursanalyse', Zeitschrift für Semiotik, vol. 35, 3-4, 353–391

Weishaupt, Martin (1913) Ostafrikanische Wandertage: Durch das Gebiet der Leipziger Mission in Deutsch-Ostafrika, Leipzig

Weishaupt, Martin (1916) Gottes Spuren im afrikanischen Bergland: Bilder aus der Leipziger Missionsarbeit in Ostafrika, 4th edn, Leipzig

Weishaupt, Martin (1925) Gottes Spuren im afrikanischen Bergland: Bilder aus der Leipziger Missionsarbeit in Ostafrika, Leipzig

Wollmershäuser, Friedrich R. (1972) Aus der Enge in die Weite: Geschichte der Familie Dillenius, Stuttgart

Zilz, Walther (1927) Theodor Wangemann oder aus der Enge in die Weite, Konstanz

Authors

Kristina Ecis is a PhD student at the University of Latvia. Her research interests include mission history in Latvia. She has studied missiology at the International Baptist Theological Seminary and theology and science of religions at the University of Latvia. She is a lecturer at the University of the Nations and Latvian Biblical Centre.

Dr. Moritz Fischer is a Professor of "World Christianities and Mission History" at the University of Applied Science for Intercultural Theology (FIT) in Hermannsburg. He earned his doctorate in Mission Science / Religious Studies at Heidelberg University (2000), presenting a thesis on Inculturation of the Gospel among the Maasai in East Africa. His habilitation was done at Augustana-University in Neuendettelsau (2011) from a social-anthropological point of view with a research on a worldwide entangled Pentecostal migrant church with its history and theology, inaugurated in the DR Congo. Fischer edited the volume "Investigations on the 'Entangled History' of Colonialism and Mission in a new perspective" (Berlin 2022).

Konstantin Gerber studied theology and cultural anthropology in Berlin and Halle (Saale) (BA). At the Martin Luther University Halle/Wittenberg he worked as a student assistant in the seminar for missiology and intercultural theology. In his research he focuses primarily on the influence of postcolonial theories on contemporary theology. He works in political education work in international exchange programs.

Jürgen Günther is a retired pastor. He worked in the regional church in Braunschweig/ Lower Saxony from 1987 to 2016. He studied Protestant theology in Hamburg with a focus on ecumenism and mission and completed a master's degree in theology with a thesis on the German Baptist mission in the colonial context of Cameroon.

Gladson Jathanna is the Assistant Professor of History of Christianities at Drew University Theological School, New Jersey/USA. He is an alumnus of George August University, Goettingen/Germany, and a former teaching faculty at Gurukul, Chennai/India and Pacific Theological College in Suva/Fiji Islands.

Emmanuel Majola is the Headmaster of the Ailanga Lutheran Junior Seminary, Meru Diocese, Tanzania. He studied theology (BD) at Makumira Lutheran Theological College in Arusha and has a Post Graduate Diploma in Education (PGDE) from Arusha University, and also a Master of Art in Education Management (MAED) from Tumaini University Makumira, Arusha.

Moni Parisius is a graduate with a Bachelor's degree in Intercultural Theology, Migration, and Global Cooperation from the University of Applied Sciences for Intercultural Theology in Hermannsburg. In 2020/2021, they undertook a valuable internship at Leipzig Mission. Currently based in Leipzig, Moni is working in the field of special education.

Dr. Joseph W. Parsalaw is an Associate Professor of Church History teaching at Tumaini University Makumira in Tanzania. He is also the Vice Chancellor of Tumaini University Makumira. His Doctorate of Theology was earned in Church History at Erlangen University, Germany, in 1997, under the late Professor Niels Peter Moritzen.

Ravinder Salooja is a mission theologian, pastor & church manager. Presently he works as chaplain at Tübingen university. From 2016-2022 he served as Director of Leipzig Mission, the successor organization of Leipzig Evangelical Lutheran Mission Society.

Dr. Karolin Wetjen is an Assistant Professor of Modern History at the University of Göttingen. She earned her doctorate in Modern History at Göttingen University in 2019, presenting a thesis on negotiations of Religion in East Africa at the end of the 19th century, utilizing the Leipzig Mission as a key example. In collaboration with Linda Ratschiller, Dr. Wetjen co-edited a volume on new approaches in mission history titled "Verflochtene Mission: Perspektiven auf eine neue Missionsgeschichte" (Cologne 2018).

Climbing high mountains
Colonial entanglement & postcolonial reflections

Preparatory session in German language only:

Thursday 28 October, 2021: 18:00 CEST (UTC+2)

Mission im kolonialen Kontext. Karl von Schwartz und der Eintritt (der Leipziger Mission) in die Kolonie Deutsch-Ostafrika, Geschichtswerkstatt (History workshop) with Jürgen Günther (DE)

Friday 29 October, 2021 – 16:00-20:00 h CEST (UTC+2)

15:45   Technical support / opening of the ZOOM session

16:00   **Welcome Address**
Rev. Daniel Keiling, Tanzania Secretary Leipzig Mission

Introduction
Rev. Ravinder Salooja, Director Leipzig Mission

16:30   **Colonisation, conversion, and co-option: Postcolonial reflections**
Dr. Gladson Jathanna, Senior Lecturer, Department of History of Christianity, Pacific Theological College, Suva, Fiji

17:30   **Mission – white, western, colonial? Mission in the contemporary theological discourse in Germany**
Konstantin Gerber, Martin Luther University Halle-Wittenberg, Faculty of Theology

18:00   Break

18:15   **Unavoidably entangled into the machinery of war? Missionaries squeezed between their supposed African addressees and the German colonial military**
Prof. Dr. Moritz Fischer, University of Applied Sciences for Intercultural Theology,
Südheide-Hermannsburg

19:15   **Evening prayer**
Rev. Daniel Keiling and Rev. Emmanuel Majola

20:00   Closing

Saturday 30 October, 2021 – 9:00-13:00 h CEST (UTC+2)

09:00 Welcome

09:05 **Morning prayer**

09:20 **The geographical and chronological perspectives of Leipziq Missionaries' activities, around Meru land for about 125 years ago**
Rev. Emmanuel Majola, Head of Ailanga Lutheran Junior Seminary, Meru Diocese, Tanzania

10:00 **The Akeri Killings of 1896**
Prof. Dr. Joseph W. Parsalaw, Vice Chancellor, Tumaini University Makumira

11:00 Break

11:15 **125 years death at Mt. Meru. A discourse analysis of the reception of the killing of two Leipzig missionaries from a postcolonial perspective**
Moni Parisius, University of Applied Sciences for Intercultural Theology, Südheide-Hermannsburg

Rediscovery and reevaluation of mission understanding of the Courland Lutheran Consistory and missionary martyr Karl Segebrock
Kristina Ecis, University of Latvia, Faculty of Theology, Riga

12:20 **Lessons learned**
Discussion started with 5 points by *Dr. Karolin Wetjen*, Assistant Professor, University Kassel, Faculty of Social Sciences

final plenary discussion

12:45 **Thanks & Farewell**
Antje Lanzendorf, Communications Manager Leipzig Mission

13:00 Closing

E-Mail by Mari-Ann Oviir in the name of the family to Leipzig Mission

Greetings from family Oviir on the 125th anniversary of Evald Ovir's passing

The month of October is dedicated to missionary work in the Estonian church calendar. Missionary Day is usually held on the fourth Sunday of October. This is connected to Evald Ovir and Karl Segebrock's martyrdom on October 20th, 1896.

The main task of the church is to do missionary work. Every era that Christians go through has its own challenges, but the call is the same. These challenges should not discourage the hope within us that the faith is continuously calling us for. In the spiritual sense, we're perhaps facing a season of drought, but with the hope in God, the missionary work will always be fruitful. The life and challenges of Christians today can still be compared to the life of Christians who lived centuries before us. The word of God is the source of strength and power for the congregation and for the missionary work in general. If we read the Word and follow it in honest belief, human relationships are transformed, broken souls are healed and new hope is born in complicated situations. The main aim of the missionary work is not to grow in numbers, but rather to maintain and pass on the ethical values to the next generations. On the stormy sea that is our life, we are all searching for light to survive. In this sense Christianity is like a beacon to us. It shows us the way, which is paramount to Christianity.

So did also Evald Ovir and Karl Segebrock act as kind of beacons doing their missionary work in East Africa. The missionaries didn't just announce the gospel in Africa. They also contributed to public education. Evald Julius Ovir was born in 1873 at Jõelähtme and died in 1896 as a martyr in Arusha, East Africa. As a result of his dedicated work, Evald Ovir managed to gather over 3000 kijagga words and expressions and explore the Swahili language.

Pastor Madis Oviir has studied thoroughly Evald Ovir's life and activities and wrote a couple hundred pages long overview of it. Neither has the younger generation forgotten about Evald Ovir. They've been several times on the tombs of Evald Ovir and Karl Segebrock. Deep respect to all who've been taking care of their tombs from our part.

It is symbolic that the Oviir forefathers got their name from the Bible and it has multiple meanings.

Bible verses that mention forgiveness lay a great foundation for missionary work. "Forgive each other". Forgiveness has a great influence on human relationships and also to the relationships of nations and countries. The power of forgiveness is God's gift to us. In its liberating power we can feel the oneness with each other and with God - it has an eternal dimension.

God bless you and give you the power of the Holy Spirit to follow Jesus.

In the name of family Oviir,
Mari-Ann Oviir
Tallinn, 7 October 2021